Hello, Android

Introducing Google's
Mobile Development Platform

Hello, Android

Introducing Google's
Mobile Development Platform

Ed Burnette

The Pragmatic Bookshelf
Raleigh, North Carolina   Dallas, Texas

Many of the designations used by manufacturers and sellers to distinguish their products are claimed as trademarks. Where those designations appear in this book, and The Pragmatic Programmers, LLC was aware of a trademark claim, the designations have been printed in initial capital letters or in all capitals. The Pragmatic Starter Kit, The Pragmatic Programmer, Pragmatic Programming, Pragmatic Bookshelf and the linking g device are trademarks of The Pragmatic Programmers, LLC.

Portions of the book's cover are reproduced from work created and shared by Google and used according to terms described in the Creative Commons 2.5 Attribution License. See http://code.google.com/policies.html#restrictions for details.

Every precaution was taken in the preparation of this book. However, the publisher assumes no responsibility for errors or omissions, or for damages that may result from the use of information (including program listings) contained herein.

Our Pragmatic courses, workshops, and other products can help you and your team create better software and have more fun. For more information, as well as the latest Pragmatic titles, please visit us at

> http://www.pragprog.com

Printed in the United States of America.

ISBN-10: 1-934356-17-4

ISBN-13: 978-1-934356-17-3

Printed on acid-free paper.

P1.0 printing, December 2008

Version: 2008-12-5

Contents

Acknowledgments

I'd like to thank the many people who made this book possible, including my reviewers Anthony Stevens, Gabor Paller, Fred Burke, Dianne Hackborn, and Laurent Pontier for their attention to detail; my editor Susannah Pfalzer for her great suggestions and good cheer in the face of impossible deadlines; and especially my family for their patience in putting up with all the long hours.

Preface

Android is a new open source software toolkit for mobile phones that was created by Google and the Open Handset Alliance. In a few years, it's expected to be found in millions of cell phones and other mobile devices, making Android a major platform for application developers. Whether you're a hobbyist or a professional programmer, whether you are doing it for fun or for profit, it's time to learn more about developing for Android. This book will help you get started.

What Makes Android Special?

There are already many mobile platforms on the market today, including Symbian, iPhone, Windows Mobile, BlackBerry, Java Mobile Edition, Linux Mobile (LiMo), and more. When I tell people about Android, their first question is often, Why do we need another mobile standard? Where's the "wow"?

Although some of its features have appeared before, Android is the first environment that combines the following:

- *A truly open, free development platform based on Linux and open source*: Handset makers like it because they can use and customize the platform without paying a royalty. Developers like it because they know that the platform "has legs" and is not locked into any one vendor that may go under or be acquired.

- *A component-based architecture inspired by Internet mashups*: Parts of one application can be used in another in ways not originally envisioned by the developer. You can even replace built-in components with your own improved versions. This will unleash a new round of creativity in the mobile space.

- *Tons of built-in services out of the box*: Location-based services use GPS or cell tower triangulation to let you customize the user experience depending on where you are. A full-powered SQL database lets you harness the power of local storage for occasionally connected computing and synchronization. Browser and map views can be embedded directly in your applications. All these built-in capabilities help raise the bar on functionality while lowering your development costs.

- *Automatic management of the application life cycle*: Programs are isolated from each other by multiple layers of security, which will provide a level of system stability not seen before in smart phones. The end user will no longer have to worry about what applications are active or close some programs so that others can run. Android is optimized for low-power, low-memory devices in a fundamental way that no previous platform has attempted.

- *High-quality graphics and sound*: Smooth, antialiased 2D vector graphics and animation inspired by Flash are melded with 3D accelerated OpenGL graphics to enable new kinds of games and business applications. Codecs for the most common industry-standard audio and video formats are built right in, including H.264 (AVC), MP3, and AAC.

- *Portability across a wide range of current and future hardware*: All your programs are written in Java and executed by Android's Dalvik virtual machine, so your code will be portable across ARM, x86, and other architectures. Support for a variety of input methods is included such as keyboard, touch, and trackball. User interfaces can be customized for any screen resolution and orientation.

Android offers a fresh take on the way mobile applications interact with users, along with the technical underpinnings to make it possible. But the best part of Android is the software that you are going to write for it. This book will help you get off to a great start.

Who Should Read This Book?

The only requirement is a basic understanding of programming in Java or a similar object-oriented language (C# will do in a pinch). You don't need any prior experience developing software for mobile devices. In fact, if you do, it's probably best if you try to forget that experience. Android is so different that it's good to start with an open mind.

What's in This Book?

Hello, Android is divided into three parts. Roughly speaking, the book progresses from less advanced to more advanced topics, or from more common to less common aspects of Android.

Several chapters share a common example: an Android Sudoku game. By gradually adding features to the game, you'll learn about many aspects of Android programming including user interfaces, multimedia, and the Android life cycle.

In Part I, we'll start with an introduction to Android. This is where you'll learn how to install the Android emulator and how to use an integrated development environment (IDE) to write your first program. Then we'll introduce a few key concepts like the Android life cycle. Programming in Android is a little different from what you're probably used to, so make sure you get these concepts before moving on.

Part II talks about Android's user interface, two-dimensional graphics, multimedia components, and simple data access. These features will be used in most programs you write.

Part III digs deeper into the Android platform. Here you'll learn about connecting to the outside world, location-based services, the built-in SQLite database, and three-dimensional graphics.

At the end of the book, you'll find an appendix that covers the differences between Android and Java Standard Edition (SE).

Online Resources

At the website for this book, http://pragprog.com/titles/eband, you'll find the following:

- The full source code for all the sample programs used in this book

- An errata page, listing any mistakes in the current edition (let's hope that will be empty!)

- A discussion forum where you can communicate directly with the author and other Android developers (let's hope that will be full!)

You are free to use the source code in your own applications as you see fit. Note: If you're reading the PDF version of this book, you can also click the little gray rectangle before the code listings to download that source file directly.

Fast-Forward >>

Although most authors expect you to read every word in their books, I know you're not going to do that. You want to read just enough to let you get something done, and then maybe you'll come back later and read something else to let you get another piece done. So, I've tried to provide you with a little help so you won't get lost.

Each chapter in this book ends with a "Fast-Forward >> section." These sections will provide some guidance for where you should go next when you need to read the book out of order. You'll also find pointers to other resources such as books and online documentation here in case you want to learn more about the subject.

So, what are you waiting for? The next chapter—Chapter 1, *Quick Start*, on page 3—drops you right into the deep end with your first Android program. Chapter 2, *Key Concepts*, on page 11 takes a step back and introduces you to the basic concepts and philosophy of Android, and Chapter 3, *Designing the User Interface*, on page 27 digs into the user interface, which will be the most important part of most Android programs.

Part I

Introducing Android

Chapter 1

Quick Start

Android combines the ubiquity of cell phones, the excitement of open source software, and the corporate backing of Google and other Open Handset Alliance members like Intel, TI, T-Mobile, and NTT DoCoMo. The result is a mobile platform you can't afford *not* to learn.

Luckily, getting started developing with Android is easy. You don't even need access to an Android phone—just a computer where you can install the Android SDK and phone emulator.

In this chapter, I'll show you how to get all the development tools installed, and then we'll jump right in and create a working application: Android's version of "Hello, World."

1.1 Installing the Tools

The Android software development kit (SDK) works on Windows, Linux, and Mac OS X. The applications you create, of course, can be deployed on any Android devices.

Before you start coding, you need to install Java, an IDE, and the Android SDK.

Java 5.0+

First you need a copy of Java. All the Android development tools require it, and programs you write will be using the Java language. JDK 5 or 6 is required.

It's not enough to just have a runtime environment (JRE); you need the full development kit. I recommend getting the latest Sun JDK 6.0

update from the Sun download site.[1] Mac OS X users should get the latest version of Mac OS X and the JDK from the Apple website.

To verify you have the right version, run this command from your shell window. Here's what I get when I run it:

```
C:\> java -version
java version "1.6.0_02"
Java(TM) SE Runtime Environment (build 1.6.0_02-b05)
Java HotSpot(TM) Client VM (build 1.6.0_02-b05, mixed mode)
```

You should see something similar, with version "1.6.something" or later.

Eclipse

Next, you should install a Java development environment if you don't have one already. I recommend Eclipse, because it's free and because it's used and supported by the Google developers who created Android.

If you don't want to use Eclipse (there's always one in every crowd), support for other IDEs such as NetBeans and JetBrains IDEA is available from their respective communities. Or if you're really old-school, you can forgo an IDE entirely and just use the command-line tools.[2]

The minimum version of Eclipse is 3.3.1, but you should always use whatever is the most up-to-date production version. Note that you need more than just the standard Eclipse SDK "classic" platform. Go to the Eclipse downloads page,[3] and pick "Eclipse IDE for Java Developers." Follow the directions there for downloading, unpacking, and installing Eclipse into a suitable location (like C:\Eclipse on Windows).

Android

Next, download the latest Android SDK from Google. The Android download page[4] has packages for Windows, Mac OS X, and Linux. After downloading the package that's right for you, unpack the .zip file to a convenient directory (for example, C:\Google).

By default, the SDK will be expanded into a subdirectory like android-sdk-windows-1.0_r1. This is your *SDK install directory*; make a note of the full path so you can refer to it later.

---

1. http://java.sun.com/javase/downloads
2. See http://code.google.com/android/intro/tools.html for documentation on the command-line tools.
3. http://www.eclipse.org/downloads
4. http://code.google.com/android/download.html

> **Powered by Pulse**
>
> For an easier Eclipse download experience, you could try the new Pulse site,* sponsored by Genuitec. You can get the Android SDK from there too with a few clicks. Pulse downloads are smaller and faster than regular Eclipse.org downloads, and you don't have to mess with .zip files. However, you may experience trouble with the site if you're behind a corporate firewall.
>
> ---
> *. http://www.poweredbypulse.com

No special install program is needed. The next step is to start Eclipse and configure it.

Eclipse Plug-In

To make development easier, Google has written a plug-in for Eclipse called the Android Development Toolkit (ADT). To install the plug-in, follow these steps (note these directions are for Eclipse 3.4—different versions may have slightly different menus and options):

1. Start Eclipse, and select Help > Software Updates....

2. Click the Available Software tab if it's not already selected.

3. Click the Add Site... button.

4. Enter the location of the Android update site: https://dl-ssl.google.com/android/eclipse/.

    Once you've filled it out, the dialog box should look like Figure 1.1, on the next page. Click OK.

5. The Android site should now appear in the Available Software view. Select the checkbox next to it, and then click Install.... If you get an error message, then you may not have the right version of Eclipse. I strongly recommend using either the prebuilt Eclipse IDE for Java or the Eclipse IDE for Java EE Development packages, version 3.4 or newer.

    If you have a custom install of Eclipse, then to use the Android editors you will also need to install the Web Standard Tools (WST) plug-in and all its prerequisites.

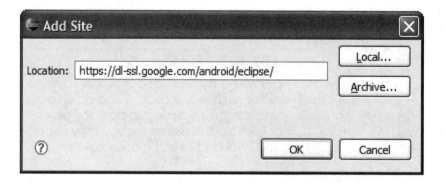

Figure 1.1: INSTALLING THE ANDROID DEVELOPMENT TOOLKIT

See the Web Tools platform home page[5] for more details and download links. These are already built into the recommended packages mentioned earlier.

6. Click Finish to start the download and install process.

7. Once the install is done, restart Eclipse.

8. When Eclipse comes back up, you may see a few error messages because you need to tell it where the Android SDK is located. Select Window > Preferences > Android, and enter the SDK install directory you noted earlier. Click OK.

Whew! Luckily, you have to do that only once (or at least once every time a new version of ADT or Eclipse comes out). Now that everything is installed, it's time to write your first program.

1.2 Creating Your First Program

ADT comes with a built-in example program, or template, that we're going to use to create a simple "Hello, Android" program in just a few seconds. Get your stopwatch ready. Ready? Set? Go!

Select File > New > Android Project to open the New Project dialog box. Then select Android > Android Project, and click Next.

---

5. http://www.eclipse.org/webtools

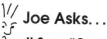 **Joe Asks...**

It Says "Connection Error." So Now What?

If you get a connection error, the most likely cause is some kind of firewall erected by your system administrators. To get outside the firewall, you'll need to configure Eclipse with the address of your proxy server. This is the same proxy server you use for your web browser, but unfortunately Eclipse isn't smart enough to pick up the setting from there.

To tell Eclipse about the proxy, select Window > Preferences > Network Connections, turn on the option for Manual proxy configuration, enter the server name and port number, and click OK. If you don't see the option, you may be running an older version of Eclipse. Try looking under Preferences > Install/Update, or search the preferences for the word *proxy*.

Enter the following information:

```
Project name: Hello
Package name: org.example.hello
Activity name: Hello
Application name: Hello, Android
```

When you're done, it should look something like Figure 1.2, on the following page.

Click Finish. The Android plug-in will create the project and fill it in with some default files. Eclipse will build it and package it up so it will be ready to execute.

OK, that takes care of writing the program; now all that's left is to try running it.

1.3 Running on the Emulator

To run your Android program, go to the Package Explorer window, right-click the HelloAndroid project, and select Run As > Android Application. This causes the Android emulator window to start up and boot the Android operating system. The first time you do this, it may take a minute or two, so be patient. If you see an error message saying that the application is not responding, select the option to continue waiting.

Figure 1.2: NEW ANDROID PROJECT

> **Shortening the Turnaround**
>
> Starting the emulator is expensive. Think about it this way—when you first turn on your phone, it needs to boot up just like any computer system. Closing the emulator is just like turning off the phone or pulling the batteries out. So, don't turn it off!
>
> Leave the emulator window running as long as Eclipse is running. The next time you start an Android program, Eclipse will notice the emulator is already there and will just send it the new program to run.

After the emulator window starts, Eclipse will send it a copy of your program to execute. The application screen comes up, and your "Hello, Android" program is now running (see Figure 1.3, on the next page). That's it! Congratulations on your first Android program.

1.4 Running on a Real Phone

Running an Android program on a physical device such as the T-Mobile G1 during development is almost identical to running it on the emulator. All you need to do is connect your phone to the computer with a USB cable and install a special device driver.[6] Close the emulator window if it's already open. As long as the phone is plugged in, applications will be loaded and run there instead.

When you're ready to publish your application for others to use, you'll need to obtain a cryptographic key and use it to sign your package. Detailed instructions for that are available online.[7] For a small registration fee you can then upload your programs to the Android Market.[8] Having your application listed on the Market is your ultimate goal. Millions of users from around the world will be able to read about your work, rate it, and even purchase it.[9]

---

6. You can find the device driver and installation instructions at http://code.google.com/android/intro/develop-and-debug.html#developingondevicehardware.
7. http://code.google.com/android/devel/sign-publish.html
8. http://market.android.com
9. According to Google, paid application support is scheduled for early 2009. Before then, all programs listed on the Android Market are free.

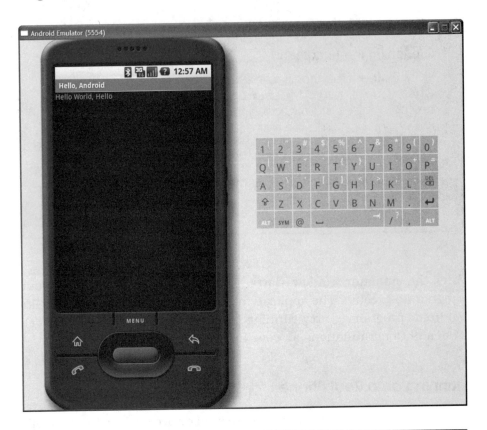

Figure 1.3: RUNNING THE "HELLO, ANDROID" PROGRAM

1.5 Fast-Forward >>

Thanks to the Eclipse plug-in, creating a skeletal Android program takes only a few seconds. In Chapter 3, *Designing the User Interface*, on page 27, we'll begin to flesh out that skeleton with a real application—a Sudoku game. This sample will be used in several chapters to demonstrate Android's API.

But before delving into that, you should take a few minutes to read Chapter 2, *Key Concepts*, on the next page. Once you grasp the basic concepts such as activities and life cycles, the rest will be much easier to understand.

Although the use of Eclipse to develop Android programs is optional, I highly recommend it. If you've never used Eclipse before, you may want to invest in a quick reference such as the *Eclipse IDE Pocket Guide* [Bur05].

Key Concepts

Now that you have an idea of what Android is, let's take a look at how it works. Some parts of Android may be familiar, such as the Linux kernel, OpenGL, and the SQL database. Others will be completely foreign, such as Android's idea of the application life cycle.

You'll need a good understanding of these key concepts in order to write well-behaved Android applications, so if you read only one chapter in this book, read this one.

2.1 The Big Picture

Let's start by taking a look at the overall system architecture—the key layers and components that make up the Android open source software stack. In Figure 2.1, on the following page, you can see the "20,000-foot" view of Android. Study it closely—there will be a test tomorrow.

Each layer uses the services provided by the layers below it. Starting from the bottom, the following sections highlight the layers provided by Android.

Linux Kernel

Android is built on top of a solid and proven foundation: the Linux kernel. Created by Linus Torvalds in 1991 while he was a student at the University of Helsinki, Linux can be found today in everything from wristwatches to supercomputers. Linux provides the hardware abstraction layer for Android, allowing Android to be ported to a wide variety of platforms in the future.

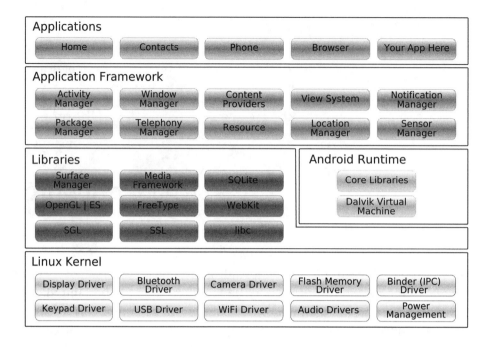

Figure 2.1: ANDROID SYSTEM ARCHITECTURE

Internally, Android uses Linux for its memory management, process management, networking, and other operating system services. The Android phone user will never see Linux, and your programs will not make Linux calls directly. As a developer, though, you'll need to be aware it's there.

Some utilities you need during development interact with Linux. For example, the adb shell command[1] will open a Linux shell in which you can enter other commands to run on the device. From there you can examine the Linux file system, view active processes, and so forth.

Native Libraries

The next layer above the kernel contains the Android native libraries. These shared libraries are all written in C or C++, compiled for the particular hardware architecture used by the phone, and preinstalled by the phone vendor.

---

1. http://code.google.com/android/reference/adb.html

Some of the most important native libraries include the following:

- *Surface Manager*: Android uses a compositing window manager similar to Vista or Compiz, but it's much simpler. Instead of drawing directly to the screen buffer, your drawing commands go into offscreen bitmaps that are then combined with other bitmaps to form the display the user sees. This lets the system create all sorts of interesting effects such as see-through windows and fancy transitions.

- *2D and 3D graphics*: Two- and three-dimensional elements can be combined in a single user interface with Android. The library will use 3D hardware if the device has it or a fast software renderer if it doesn't. See Chapter 4, *Exploring 2D Graphics*, on page 57 and Chapter 10, *3D Graphics in OpenGL*, on page 181.

- *Media codecs*: Android can play video and record and play back audio in a variety of formats including AAC, AVC (H.264), H.263, MP3, and MPEG-4. See Chapter 5, *Multimedia*, on page 89 for an example.

- *SQL database*: Android includes the lightweight SQLite database engine,[2] the same database used in Firefox and the Apple iPhone. You can use this for persistent storage in your application. See Chapter 9, *Putting SQL to Work*, on page 161 for an example.

- *Browser engine*: For the fast display of HTML content, Android uses the WebKit library.[3] This is the same engine used in the Google Chrome browser, Apple's Safari browser, the Apple iPhone, and Nokia's S60 platform. See Chapter 7, *The Connected World*, on page 117 for an example.

Android Runtime

Also sitting on top of the kernel is the Android runtime, including the Dalvik virtual machine and the core Java libraries.

The Dalvik VM is Google's implementation of Java, optimized for mobile devices. All the code you write for Android will be written in Java and run within the VM.

---

2. http://www.sqlite.org
3. http://www.webkit.org

> \\\// Joe Asks...
> ~,~
> ~ __What's a Dalvik?__
>
> Dalvik is a virtual machine (VM) designed and written by Dan Bornstein at Google. Your code gets compiled into machine-independent instructions called *bytecodes*, which are then executed by the Dalvik VM on the mobile device.
>
> Although the bytecode formats are a little different, Dalvik is essentially a Java virtual machine optimized for low memory requirements. It allows multiple VM instances to run at once and takes advantage of the underlying operating system (Linux) for security and process isolation.
>
> Bornstein named Dalvik after a fishing village in Iceland where some of his ancestors lived.

Dalvik differs from traditional Java in two important ways:

- The Dalvik VM runs .dex files, which are converted at compile time from standard .class and .jar files. .dex files are more compact and efficient than class files, an important consideration for the limited memory and battery-powered devices that Android targets.

- The core Java libraries that come with Android are different from both the Java Standard Edition (Java SE) libraries and the Java Mobile Edition (Java ME) libraries. There is a substantial amount of overlap, however. In Appendix A, on page 207, you'll find a comparison of Android and standard Java libraries.

Application Framework

Sitting above the native libraries and runtime, you'll find the Application Framework layer. This layer provides the high-level building blocks you will use to create your applications. The framework comes preinstalled with Android, but you can also extend it with your own components as needed.

The most important parts of the framework are as follows:

- *Activity manager*: This controls the life cycle of applications (see Section 2.2, *It's Alive!*, on page 16) and maintains a common "backstack" for user navigation.

> ### Embrace and Extend
>
> One of the unique and powerful qualities of Android is that all applications have a level playing field. What I mean is that the system applications have to go through the same public API that you use. You can even tell Android to make your application replace the standard applications if you want.

- *Content providers*: These objects encapsulate data that needs to be shared between applications, such as contacts. See Section 2.3, *Content Providers*, on page 21.

- *Resource manager*: Resources are anything that goes with your program that is not code. See Section 2.4, *Using Resources*, on page 21.

- *Location manager*: An Android phone always knows where it is. See Chapter 8, *Locating and Sensing*, on page 145.

- *Notification manager*: Events such as arriving messages, appointments, proximity alerts, alien invasions, and more can be presented in an unobtrusive fashion to the user.

Applications

The highest layer in the Android architecture diagram is the Applications layer. Think of this as the tip of the Android iceberg. End users will see only these applications, blissfully unaware of all the action going on below the waterline. As an Android developer, however, you know better.

When someone buys an Android phone, it will come prepackaged with a number of standard system applications, including the following:

- Phone dialer
- Email
- Contacts
- Web browser
- Android Market

Using the Android Market, the user will be able to download new programs to run on their phone. That's where you come in. By the time you finish this book, you'll be able to write your own killer applications for Android.

Now let's take a closer look at the life cycle of an Android application. It's a little different from what you're used to seeing.

2.2 It's Alive!

On your standard Linux or Windows desktop, you can have many applications running and visible at once in different windows. One of the windows has keyboard focus, but otherwise all the programs are equal. You can easily switch between them, but it's your responsibility as the user to move the windows around so you can see what you're doing and close programs you don't need anymore.

Android doesn't work that way.

In Android, there is one foreground application, which typically takes over the whole display except for the status line. When the user turns on their phone, the first application they see is the Home application (see Figure 2.2, on the next page). This program typically shows the time, a background image, and a scrollable list of other applications the user can invoke.

When the user runs an application, Android starts it and brings it to the foreground. From that application, the user might invoke another application, or another screen in the same application, and then another and another. All these programs and screens are recorded on the *application stack* by the system's Activity Manager. At any time, the user can press the Back button to return to the previous screen on the stack. From the user's point of view, it works a lot like the history in a web browser. Pressing Back returns them to the previous page.

Process != Application

Internally, each user interface screen is represented by an Activity class (see Section 2.3, *Activities*, on page 20). Each activity has its own life cycle. An application is one or more activities plus a Linux process to contain them. That sounds pretty straightforward, doesn't it? But don't get comfortable yet; I'm about to throw you a curve ball.

Figure 2.2: THE HOME APPLICATION

In Android, an application can be "alive" even if its process has been killed. Put another way, the activity life cycle is not tied to the process life cycle. Processes are just disposable containers for activities. This is probably different from every other system you're familiar with, so let's take a closer look before moving on.

Life Cycles of the Rich and Famous

During its lifetime, each activity of an Android program can be in one of several states, as shown in Figure 2.3, on the next page. You, the developer, do not have control over what state your program is in. That's all managed by the system. However, you do get notified when the state is about to change through the on*XX*() method calls.

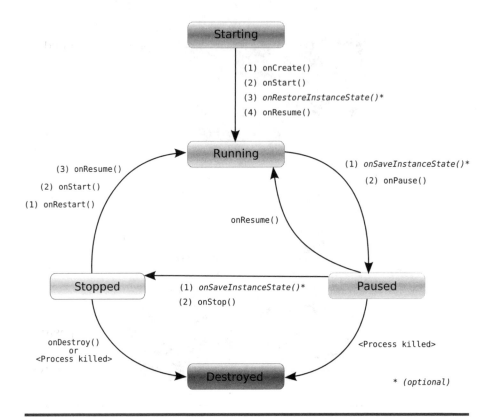

Figure 2.3: LIFE CYCLE OF AN ANDROID ACTIVITY

You override these methods in your Activity class, and Android will call them at the appropriate time:

- onCreate(Bundle): This is called when the activity first starts up. You can use it to perform one-time initialization such as creating the user interface. onCreate() takes one parameter that is either **null** or some state information previously saved by the onSaveInstanceState() method.

- onStart(): This indicates the activity is about to be displayed to the user.

- onResume(): This is called when your activity can start interacting with the user. This is a good place to start animations and music.

- onPause(): This runs when the activity is about to go into the background, usually because another activity has been launched in front of it. This is where you should save your program's persistent state, such as a database record being edited.

- onStop(): This is called when your activity is no longer visible to the user and it won't be needed for a while. If memory is tight, onStop() may never be called (the system may simply terminate your process).

- onRestart(): If this method is called, it indicates your activity is being redisplayed to the user from a stopped state.

- onDestroy(): This is called right before your activity is destroyed. If memory is tight, onDestroy() may never be called (the system may simply terminate your process).

- onSaveInstanceState(Bundle): Android will call this method to allow the activity to save per-instance state, such as a cursor position within a text field. Usually you won't need to override it because the default implementation saves the state for all your user interface controls automatically.[4]

- onRestoreInstanceState(Bundle): This is called when the activity is being reinitialized from a state previously saved by the onSaveInstanceState() method. The default implementation restores the state of your user interface.

Activities that are not running in the foreground may be stopped or the Linux process that houses them may be killed at any time in order to make room for new activities. This will be a common occurrence, so it's important that your application be designed from the beginning with this in mind. In some cases, the onPause() method may be the last method called in your activity, so that's where you should save any data you want to keep around for next time.

In addition to managing your program's life cycle, the Android framework provides a number of building blocks that you use to create your applications. Let's take a look at those next.

---

4. Before version 0.9_beta, onSaveInstanceState() was called onFreeze(), and the saved state was called an icicle. You may still see the old names in some documentation and examples.

> **Flipping the Lid**
>
> Here's a quick way to test that your state-saving code is working correctly. In current versions of Android, an orientation change (between portrait and landscape modes) will cause the system to go through the process of saving instance state, pausing, stopping, destroying, and then creating a new instance of the activity with the saved state. On the T-Mobile G1 phone, for example, flipping the lid on the keyboard will trigger this, and on the Android emulator pressing `Ctrl+F11` or the `7` or `9` key on the keypad will do it.

2.3 Building Blocks

A few objects are defined in the Android SDK that every developer needs to be familiar with. The most important ones are activities, intents, services, and content providers. You'll see several examples of them in the rest of the book, so I'd like to briefly introduce them now.

Activities

An *activity* is a user interface screen. Applications can define one or more activities to handle different phases of the program. As discussed in Section 2.2, *It's Alive!*, on page 16, each activity is responsible for saving its own state so that it can be restored later as part of the application life cycle. See Section 3.3, *Creating the Opening Screen*, on page 29 for an example.

Intents

An *intent* is a mechanism for describing a specific action, such as "pick a photo," "phone home," or "open the pod bay doors." In Android, just about everything goes through intents, so you have plenty of opportunities to replace or reuse components. See Section 3.5, *Implementing an About Box*, on page 40 for an example of an intent.

For example, there is an intent for "send an email." If your application needs to send mail, you can invoke that intent. Or if you're writing a new email application, you can register an activity to handle that intent and replace the standard mail program. The next time somebody tries to send an email, they'll get your program instead of the standard one.

Services

A *service* is a task that runs in the background without the user's direct interaction, similar to a Unix daemon. For example, consider a music player. The music may be started by an activity, but you want it to keep playing even when the user has moved on to a different program. So, the code that does the actual playing should be in a service. Later, another activity may bind to that service and tell it to switch tracks or stop playing. Android comes with many services built in, along with convenient APIs to access them.

Content Providers

A *content provider* is a set of data wrapped up in a custom API to read and write it. This is the best way to share global data *between applications*. For example, Google provides a content provider for contacts. All the information there—names, addresses, phone numbers, and so forth—can be shared by any application that wants to use it. See Section 9.5, *Using a ContentProvider*, on page 174 for an example.

2.4 Using Resources

A *resource* is a localized text string, bitmap, or other small piece of noncode information that your program needs. At build time all your resources get compiled into your application.

You will create and store your resources in the res directory inside your project. The Android resource compiler (aapt)[5] processes resources according to which subfolder they are in and the format of the file. For example, PNG and JPG format bitmaps should go in the res/drawable directory, and XML files that describe screen layouts should go in the res/layout directory.

The resource compiler compresses and packs your resources and then generates a class named R that contains identifiers you use to reference those resources in your program. This is a little different from standard Java resources, which are referenced by key strings. Doing it this way allows Android to make sure all your references are valid and saves space by not having to store all those resource keys. Eclipse uses a similar method to store and reference the resources in Eclipse plug-ins.

5. http://code.google.com/android/reference/aapt.html

We'll see an example of the code to access a resource in Chapter 3, *Designing the User Interface*, on page 27.

2.5 Safe and Secure

As mentioned earlier, every application runs in its own Linux process. The hardware forbids one process from accessing another process's memory. Furthermore, every application is assigned a specific user ID. Any files it creates cannot be read or written by other applications.

In addition, access to certain critical operations are restricted, and you must specifically ask for permission to use them in a file named Android-Manifest.xml. When the application is installed, the Package Manager either grants or doesn't grant the permissions based on certificates and, if necessary, user prompts. Here are some of the most common permissions you will need:

- INTERNET: Access the Internet.
- READ_CONTACTS: Read (but don't write) the user's contacts data.
- WRITE_CONTACTS: Write (but don't read) the user's contacts data.
- RECEIVE_SMS: Monitor incoming SMS (text) messages.
- ACCESS_COARSE_LOCATION: Use a coarse location provider such as cell towers or wifi.
- ACCESS_FINE_LOCATION: Use a more accurate location provider such as GPS.

For example, to monitor incoming SMS messages, you would specify this in the manifest file:

```
<manifest xmlns:android="http://schemas.android.com/apk/res/android"
    package="com.google.android.app.myapp" >
    <uses-permission android:name="android.permission.RECEIVE_SMS" />
</manifest>
```

Android can even restrict access to entire parts of the system. Using XML tags in AndroidManifest.xml, you can restrict who can start an activity, start or bind to a service, broadcast intents to a receiver, or access the data in a content provider. This kind of control is beyond the scope of this book, but if you want to learn more, read the online help for the Android security model.[6]

---

6. http://code.google.com/android/devel/security.html

2.6 Fast-Forward >>

The rest of this book will use all the concepts introduced in this chapter. In Chapter 3, *Designing the User Interface*, on page 27, we'll use activities and life-cycle methods to define a sample application. Chapter 4, *Exploring 2D Graphics*, on page 57 will use some of the graphics classes in the Android native libraries. Media codecs will be explored in Chapter 5, *Multimedia*, on page 89, and content providers will be covered in Chapter 9, *Putting SQL to Work*, on page 161.

Part II

Android Basics

Chapter 3

Designing the User Interface

In Chapter 1, *Quick Start*, on page 3, we used the Android Eclipse plug-in to put together a simple "Hello, Android" program in a few minutes. In Part II, we'll create a more substantial example: a Sudoku game. By gradually adding features to the game, you'll learn about many aspects of Android programming. We'll start with the user interface.

You can find all the sample code used in this book at http://pragprog. com/titles/eband. If you're reading the PDF version of this book, you can click the little gray rectangle before the code listings to download that file directly.

3.1 Introducing the Sudoku Example

Sudoku makes a great sample program for Android because the game itself is so simple. You have a grid of eighty-one tiles (nine across and nine down), and you try to fill them in with numbers so that each column, each row, and each of the three-by-three boxes contains the numbers 1 through 9 only once. When the game starts, some of the numbers (the *givens*) are already filled in. All the player has to do is supply the rest. A true Sudoku puzzle has only one unique solution.

Sudoku is usually played with pencil and paper, but computerized versions are quite popular too. With the paper version, it's easy to make a mistake early on, and when that happens, you have to go back and erase most of your work. In the Android version, you can change the tiles as often as you like without having to brush away all those pesky eraser shavings.

Sudoku Trivia

Most people think Sudoku is some kind of ancient Japanese game, but it's not. Although similar puzzles can be traced to 19th-century French magazines, most experts credit retired American architect Howard Garns with the invention of modern Sudoku. Number Place, as it was known at the time, was first published in the United States in 1979 by Dell Magazines.

Android Sudoku (see Figure 3.1, on the facing page) will also offer a few hints to take some of the grunt work out of puzzle solving. At one extreme, it could just solve the puzzle for you, but that wouldn't be any fun, would it? So, we have to balance the hints against the challenge and not make it too easy.

3.2 Designing by Declaration

User interfaces can be designed using one of two methods: procedural and declarative. *Procedural* simply means in code. For example, when you're programming a Swing application, you write Java code to create and manipulate all the user interface objects such as JFrame and JButton. Thus, Swing is procedural.

Declarative design, on the other hand, does not involve any code. When you're designing a simple web page, you use HTML, a markup language based on XML that describes what you want to see on the page, not how you want to do it. HTML is declarative.

Android tries to straddle the gap between the procedural and declarative worlds by letting you create user interfaces in either style. You can stay almost entirely in Java code, or you can stay almost entirely in XML descriptors. If you look up the documentation for any Android user interface component, you'll see both the Java APIs and the corresponding declarative XML attributes that do the same thing.

Which should you use? Either way is valid, but my advice is to use declarative XML as much as possible. The XML code is often shorter and easier to understand than the corresponding Java code, and future tools that might be developed for Android, such as GUI designers, will have an easier time working with it.

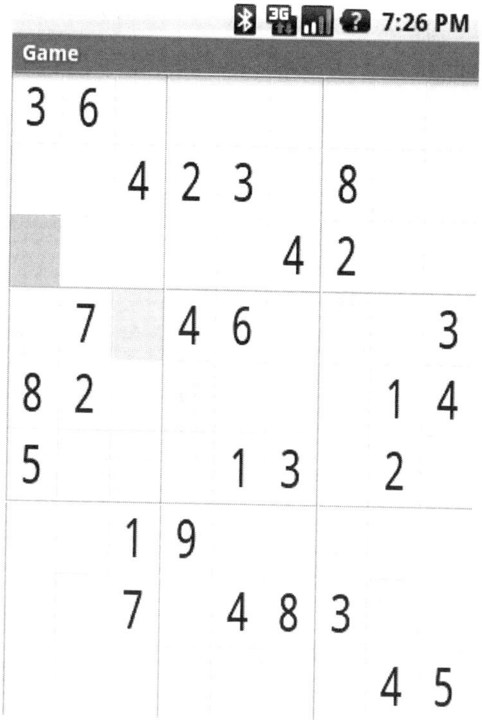

Figure 3.1: THE SUDOKU EXAMPLE PROGRAM FOR ANDROID

Now let's see how we can use this information to create the Sudoku opening screen.

3.3 Creating the Opening Screen

We'll start with a skeleton Android program created by the Eclipse plug-in. Just as you did in Section 1.2, *Creating Your First Program*, on page 6, create a new "Hello, Android" project, but this time use the following values:

```
Project name: Sudoku
Package name: org.example.sudoku
Activity name: Sudoku
Application name: Sudoku
```

In a real program, of course, you would use your own names here. The package name is particularly important. Each application in the system must have a unique package name. Once you choose a package name, it's a little tricky to change it because it's used in so many places.

I like to keep the Android emulator window up all the time and run the program after every change, since it takes only a few seconds. If you do that and run the program now, you'll see a blank screen that just contains the words "Hello World, Sudoku." The first order of business is to change that into an opening screen for the game, with buttons to let the player start a new game, continue a previous one, get information about the game, or exit. So, what do we have to change to do that?

As discussed in Chapter 2, *Key Concepts*, on page 11, Android programs are a loose collection of activities, each of which define a user interface screen. When you create the Sudoku project, the Android plug-in makes a single activity for you in Sudoku.java:

Sudokuv0/src/org/example/sudoku/Sudoku.java

```
package org.example.sudoku;

import android.app.Activity;
import android.os.Bundle;

public class Sudoku extends Activity {
    /** Called when the activity is first created. */
    @Override
    public void onCreate(Bundle savedInstanceState) {
        super.onCreate(savedInstanceState);
        setContentView(R.layout.main);
    }
}
```

Android calls the onCreate() method of your activity to initialize it. The call to setContentView() fills in the contents of the activity's screen with an Android view widget.

We could have used several lines of Java code, and possibly another class or two, to define the user interface procedurally. But instead, the plug-in chose the declarative route, and we'll continue along those lines. In the previous code, R.layout.main is a resource identifier that refers to the main.xml file in the res/layout directory (see Figure 3.2, on the next page). main.xml declares the user interface in XML, so that's the file we need to modify. At runtime, Android parses and instantiates (*inflates*) the resource defined there and sets it as the view for the current activity.

It's important to note that the R class is managed automatically by the Android Eclipse plug-in. When you put a file anywhere in the res direc-

Figure 3.2: INITIAL RESOURCES IN THE SUDOKU PROJECT

tory, the plug-in notices the change and adds resource IDs in R.java for you. If you remove or change a resource file, R.java is kept in sync. If you bring up the file in the editor, it will look something like this:

Sudokuv0/src/org/example/sudoku/R.java

```
/* AUTO-GENERATED FILE.  DO NOT MODIFY.
 *
 * This class was automatically generated by the
 * aapt tool from the resource data it found.  It
 * should not be modified by hand.
 */

package org.example.sudoku;

public final class R {
    public static final class attr {
    }
    public static final class drawable {
        public static final int icon=0x7f020000;
    }
    public static final class layout {
        public static final int main=0x7f030000;
    }
    public static final class string {
        public static final int app_name=0x7f040001;
        public static final int hello=0x7f040000;
    }
}
```

> ### Joe Asks. . .
> #### Why Does Android Use XML? Isn't That Inefficient?
>
> Android is optimized for mobile devices with limited memory and horsepower, so you may find it strange that it uses XML so pervasively. After all, XML is a verbose, human-readable format not known for its brevity or efficiency, right?
>
> Although you see XML when writing your program, the Eclipse plug-in invokes the Android resource compiler, aapt, to preprocess the XML into a compressed binary format. It is this format, not the original XML text, that is stored on the device.

The hex numbers are just integers that the Android resource manager uses to load the real data, the strings, and the other assets that are compiled into your package. You don't need to worry about their values. Just keep in mind that they are handles that refer to the data, not the objects that contain the data. Those objects won't be inflated until they are needed. Note that almost every Android program, including the base Android framework itself, has an R class. See the online documentation on android.R for all the built-in resources you can use.[1]

So, now we know we have to modify main.xml. Let's dissect the original definition to see what we have to change. Double-click main.xml in Eclipse to open it. Depending on how you have Eclipse set up, you may see either a visual layout editor or an XML editor. In current versions of ADT, the visual layout editor isn't that useful, so click main.xml or Source tab at the bottom to see the XML.

The first line of main.xml is as follows:

```
<?xml version="1.0" encoding="utf-8"?>
```

All Android XML files start with this line. It just tells the compiler that the file is XML format, in UTF-8 encoding. UTF-8 is almost exactly like regular ASCII text, except it has escape codes for non-ASCII characters such as Japanese glyphs.

---

1. http://code.google.com/android/reference/android/R.html

Next we see a reference to <*LinearLayout*>:

```
<LinearLayout
    xmlns:android="http://schemas.android.com/apk/res/android"
    android:orientation="vertical"
    android:layout_width="fill_parent"
    android:layout_height="fill_parent">
    <!-- ... -->
</LinearLayout>
```

A layout is a container for one or more child objects and a behavior to position them on the screen within the rectangle of the parent object. Here is a list of the most common layouts provided by Android:

- FrameLayout: Arranges its children so they all start at the top left of the screen. This is used for tabbed views and image switchers.
- LinearLayout: Arranges its children in a single column or row. This is the most common layout you will use.
- RelativeLayout: Arranges its children in relation to each other or to the parent. This is often used in forms.
- TableLayout: Arranges its children in rows and columns, similar to an HTML table.

Some parameters are common to all layouts:

xmlns:android="http://schemas.android.com/apk/res/android"
> Defines the XML namespace for Android. You should define this once, on the first XML tag in the file.

android:layout_width="fill_parent", android:layout_height="fill_parent"
> Takes up the entire width and height of the parent (in this case, the window). Possible values are fill_parent and wrap_content.

Inside the <*LinearLayout*> tag you'll find one child widget:

```
<TextView
    android:layout_width="fill_parent"
    android:layout_height="wrap_content"
    android:text="@string/hello" />
```

This defines a simple text label. Let's replace that with some different text and a few buttons. Here's our first attempt:

Sudokuv1/res/layout/main1.xml

```
<?xml version="1.0" encoding="utf-8"?>
<LinearLayout
    xmlns:android="http://schemas.android.com/apk/res/android"
    android:orientation="vertical"
    android:layout_width="fill_parent"
    android:layout_height="fill_parent">
```

```
  <TextView
    android:layout_width="fill_parent"
    android:layout_height="wrap_content"
    android:text="@string/main_title" />
  <Button
    android:layout_width="fill_parent"
    android:layout_height="wrap_content"
    android:text="@string/continue_label" />
  <Button
    android:layout_width="fill_parent"
    android:layout_height="wrap_content"
    android:text="@string/new_game_label" />
  <Button
    android:layout_width="fill_parent"
    android:layout_height="wrap_content"
    android:text="@string/about_label" />
  <Button
    android:layout_width="fill_parent"
    android:layout_height="wrap_content"
    android:text="@string/exit_label" />
</LinearLayout>
```

If you see warnings in the editor about missing grammar constraints (DTD or XML schema), just ignore them.

Instead of hard-coding English text into the layout file, we use the @string/*resid* syntax to refer to strings in the res/values/strings.xml file. You can have different versions of this and other resource files based on the locale or other parameters such as screen resolution and orientation. Open that file now, switch to the strings.xml tab at the bottom if necessary, and enter this:

Sudokuv1/res/values/strings.xml

```
<?xml version="1.0" encoding="utf-8"?>
<resources>
    <string name="app_name">Sudoku</string>
    <string name="main_title">Android Sudoku</string>
    <string name="continue_label">Continue</string>
    <string name="new_game_label">New Game</string>
    <string name="about_label">About</string>
    <string name="exit_label">Exit</string>
</resources>
```

When you run the program now, you should see something like Figure 3.3, on the facing page. It's readable, but it could use some cosmetic changes.

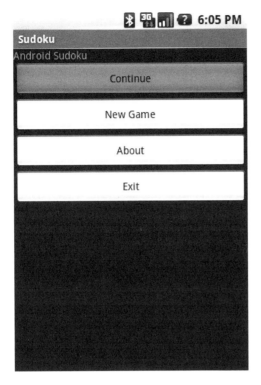

Figure 3.3: FIRST VERSION OF THE OPENING SCREEN

Let's make the title text larger and centered, make the buttons smaller, and use a different background color. Here's the color definition, which you should put in res/values/colors.xml:

Sudokuv1/res/values/colors.xml

```
<?xml version="1.0" encoding="utf-8"?>
<resources>
    <color name="background">#3500ffff</color>
</resources>
```

And here's the new layout:

Sudokuv1/res/layout/main.xml

```
<?xml version="1.0" encoding="utf-8"?>
<LinearLayout
    xmlns:android="http://schemas.android.com/apk/res/android"
    android:background="@color/background"
    android:layout_height="fill_parent"
    android:layout_width="fill_parent"
```

```
    android:padding="30dip"
    android:orientation="horizontal">
    <LinearLayout
        android:orientation="vertical"
        android:layout_height="wrap_content"
        android:layout_width="fill_parent"
        android:layout_gravity="center">
        <TextView
            android:text="@string/main_title"
            android:layout_height="wrap_content"
            android:layout_width="wrap_content"
            android:layout_gravity="center"
            android:layout_marginBottom="25dip"
            android:textSize="24.5sp" />
        <Button
            android:id="@+id/continue_button"
            android:layout_width="fill_parent"
            android:layout_height="wrap_content"
            android:text="@string/continue_label" />
        <Button
            android:id="@+id/new_button"
            android:layout_width="fill_parent"
            android:layout_height="wrap_content"
            android:text="@string/new_game_label" />
        <Button
            android:id="@+id/about_button"
            android:layout_width="fill_parent"
            android:layout_height="wrap_content"
            android:text="@string/about_label" />
        <Button
            android:id="@+id/exit_button"
            android:layout_width="fill_parent"
            android:layout_height="wrap_content"
            android:text="@string/exit_label" />
    </LinearLayout>
</LinearLayout>
```

In this version, we introduce a new syntax, @+id/*resid*. Instead of referring to a resource ID defined somewhere else, this is how you create a new resource ID to which others can refer. For example, @+id/about_button defines the ID for the About button, which we'll use later to make something happen when the user presses that button.

The result is shown in Figure 3.4, on the next page. This new screen looks good in portrait mode (when the screen is taller than it is wide), but how about landscape mode (wide-screen)? The user can switch modes at any time, for example, by flipping out the keyboard and turning the phone on its side, so you need to handle that.

Figure 3.4: Opening screen with new layout

3.4 Using Alternate Resources

As a test, try switching the emulator to landscape mode (Ctrl+F11 or the 7 or 9 key on the keypad). Oops! The Exit button runs off the bottom of the screen (see Figure 3.5, on page 39). How do we fix that?

You could try to adjust the layout so that it works with all orientations. Unfortunately, that's often not possible or leads to odd-looking screens. When that happens, you'll need to create a different layout for landscape mode. That's the approach we'll take here.

Joe Asks...

What Are Dips and Sps?

Historically, programmers always designed computer interfaces in terms of pixels. For example, you might make a field 300 pixels wide, allow 5 pixels of spacing between columns, and define icons 16-by-16 pixels in size. The problem is that if you run that program on new displays with more and more dots per inch (dpi), the user interface appears smaller and smaller. At some point, it becomes too hard to read.

Resolution-independent measurements help solve this problem. Android supports all the following units:

- **px** (pixels): Dots on the screen.

- **in** (inches): Size as measured by a ruler.

- **mm** (millimeters): Size as measured by a ruler.

- **pt** (points): 1/72 of an inch.

- **dp** (density-independent pixels): An abstract unit based on the density of the screen. On a display with 160 dots per inch, 1dp = 1px.

- **dip**: Synonym for dp, used more often in Google examples.

- **sp** (scale-independent pixels): Similar to **dp** but also scaled by the user's font size preference.

To make your interface scalable to any current and future type of display, I recommend you always use the **sp** unit for text sizes and the **dip** unit for everything else. You should also consider using vector graphics instead of bitmaps (see Chapter 4, *Exploring 2D Graphics*, on page 57).

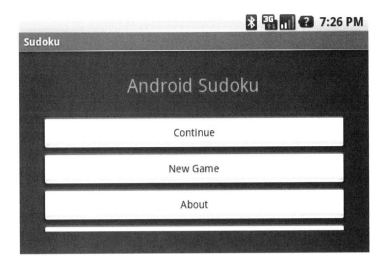

Figure 3.5: IN LANDSCAPE MODE, WE CAN'T SEE THE EXIT BUTTON.

Create a file called res/layout-land/main.xml (note the -land suffix) that contains the following layout:

Sudokuv1/res/layout-land/main.xml

```xml
<?xml version="1.0" encoding="utf-8"?>
<LinearLayout
    xmlns:android="http://schemas.android.com/apk/res/android"
    android:background="@color/background"
    android:layout_height="fill_parent"
    android:layout_width="fill_parent"
    android:padding="15dip"
    android:orientation="horizontal">
    <LinearLayout
        android:orientation="vertical"
        android:layout_height="wrap_content"
        android:layout_width="fill_parent"
        android:layout_gravity="center"
        android:paddingLeft="20dip"
        android:paddingRight="20dip">
    <TextView
        android:text="@string/main_title"
        android:layout_height="wrap_content"
        android:layout_width="wrap_content"
        android:layout_gravity="center"
        android:layout_marginBottom="20dip"
        android:textSize="24.5sp" />
```

```
<TableLayout
    android:layout_height="wrap_content"
    android:layout_width="wrap_content"
    android:layout_gravity="center"
    android:stretchColumns="*">
    <TableRow>
        <Button
            android:id="@+id/continue_button"
            android:text="@string/continue_label" />
        <Button
            android:id="@+id/new_button"
            android:text="@string/new_game_label" />
    </TableRow>
    <TableRow>
        <Button
            android:id="@+id/about_button"
            android:text="@string/about_label" />
        <Button
            android:id="@+id/exit_button"
            android:text="@string/exit_label" />
    </TableRow>
    </TableLayout>
  </LinearLayout>
</LinearLayout>
```

This uses a TableLayout to create two columns of buttons. Now run the program again (see Figure 3.6, on the facing page). Even in landscape mode, all the buttons are visible.

You can use resource suffixes to specify alternate versions of any resources, not just the layout. For example, you can use them to provide localized text strings in different languages. Each alternate resource file must define exactly the same set of IDs.

Android supports suffixes for the current language, region, pixel density, resolution, input method, and more. See the Android resources documentation for an up-to-date list of suffixes and inheritance rules.[2]

3.5 Implementing an About Box

When the user selects the About button, meaning that either they touch it (if they have a touch screen) or they navigate to it with the D-pad (directional pad) or trackball and press the selection button, we want to pop up a window with some information about Sudoku.

---

2. http://code.google.com/android/devel/resources-i18n.html#AlternateResources

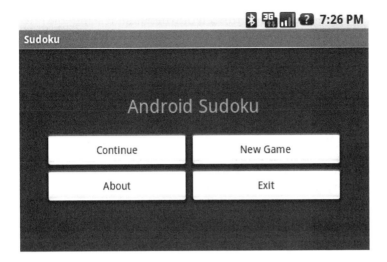

Figure 3.6: USING A LANDSCAPE-SPECIFIC LAYOUT LETS US SEE ALL THE BUTTONS.

After scrolling through the text, the user can press the Back button to dismiss the window.

We can accomplish this in several ways:

- Define a new Activity and start it.
- Use the AlertDialog class and show it.
- Subclass Android's Dialog class, and show that.

For this example, let's define a new activity. Like the main Sudoku activity, the About activity will need a layout file. We will name it res/layout/about.xml:

Sudokuv1/res/layout/about.xml

```xml
<?xml version="1.0" encoding="utf-8"?>
<ScrollView
    xmlns:android="http://schemas.android.com/apk/res/android"
    android:layout_width="fill_parent"
    android:layout_height="fill_parent"
    android:padding="10dip">
    <TextView
        android:id="@+id/about_content"
        android:layout_width="wrap_content"
        android:layout_height="wrap_content"
        android:text="@string/about_text" />
</ScrollView>
```

We need only one version of this layout because it will look fine in both portrait and landscape modes.

Now add strings for the title of the About dialog box and the text it contains to res/values/strings.xml:

Sudokuv1/res/values/strings.xml

```
<string name="about_title">About Android Sudoku</string>
<string name="about_text">\
Sudoku is a logic-based number placement puzzle.
Starting with a partially completed 9x9 grid, the
objective is to fill the grid so that each
row, each column, and each of the 3x3 boxes
(also called <i>blocks</i>) contains the digits
1 to 9 exactly once.
</string>
```

Note how a string resource can contain simple HTML formatting and can span multiple lines. In case you're wondering, the backslash character (\) in about_text prevents an extra blank from appearing before the first word.

The About activity should be defined in About.java. All it needs to do is override onCreate() and call setContentView():

Sudokuv1/src/org/example/sudoku/About.java

```
package org.example.sudoku;

import android.app.Activity;
import android.os.Bundle;

public class About extends Activity {
    @Override
    protected void onCreate(Bundle savedInstanceState) {
        super.onCreate(savedInstanceState);
        setContentView(R.layout.about);
    }
}
```

Next we need to wire all this up to the About button in the Sudoku class. Start by adding a few imports we'll need to Sudoku.java:

Sudokuv1/src/org/example/sudoku/Sudoku.java

```
import android.content.Intent;
import android.view.View;
import android.view.View.OnClickListener;
```

In the onCreate() method, add code to call findViewById() to look up an Android view given its resource ID and setOnClickListener() to tell Android which object to tickle when the user touches or clicks the view:

```
Sudokuv1/src/org/example/sudoku/Sudoku.java
/** Called when the activity is first created. */
@Override
public void onCreate(Bundle savedInstanceState) {
   super.onCreate(savedInstanceState);
   setContentView(R.layout.main);

   // Set up click listeners for all the buttons
   View continueButton = this.findViewById(R.id.continue_button);
   continueButton.setOnClickListener(this);
   View newButton = this.findViewById(R.id.new_button);
   newButton.setOnClickListener(this);
   View aboutButton = this.findViewById(R.id.about_button);
   aboutButton.setOnClickListener(this);
   View exitButton = this.findViewById(R.id.exit_button);
   exitButton.setOnClickListener(this);
}
```

While we're in here, we do the same for all the buttons. Recall that constants like R.id.about_button are created by the Eclipse plug-in in R.java when it sees @+id/about_button in res/layout/main.xml.

The code uses this as the receiver, so the Sudoku class needs to implement the OnClickListener interface and define a method called onClick:[3]

```
Sudokuv1/src/org/example/sudoku/Sudoku.java
public class Sudoku extends Activity implements OnClickListener {
   // ...
   public void onClick(View v) {
      switch (v.getId()) {
      case R.id.about_button:
         Intent i = new Intent(this, About.class);
         startActivity(i);
         break;
      // More buttons go here (if any) ...
      }
   }
}
```

To start an activity in Android, we first need to create an instance of the Intent class. There are two kinds of intents: *public* (named) intents

---

3. We could have used an anonymous inner class to handle clicks, but according to the Android developers, every new inner class takes up an extra 1KB of memory.

Figure 3.7: MOUNTAIN VIEW, WE HAVE A PROBLEM

that are registered with the system and can be called from any application and *private* (anonymous) intents that are used within a single application. For this example, we just need the latter kind.

If you run the program and select the About button now, you will get an error (see Figure 3.7). What happened?

We forgot one important step: every activity needs to be declared in AndroidManifest.xml. To do that, double-click the file to open it, switch to XML mode if necessary by selecting the AndroidManifest.xml tab at the bottom, and add a new <*activity*> tag after the closing tag of the first one:

`Sudokuv1/AndroidManifest.first.xml`

```
<activity android:name=".About"
        android:label="@string/about_title">
</activity>
```

Now if you save the manifest, run the program again, and select the About button, you should see something like Figure 3.8, on the facing page. Press the Back button ([Esc] on the emulator) when you're done.

That looks OK, but wouldn't it be nice if we could see the initial screen behind the About text?

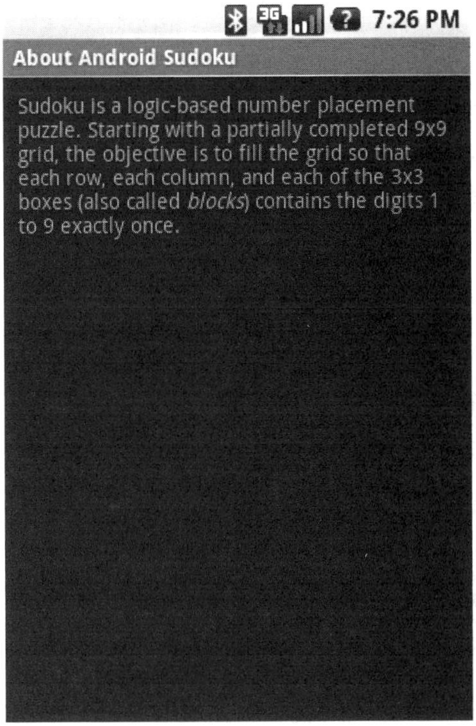

Figure 3.8: FIRST VERSION OF THE ABOUT SCREEN

3.6 Applying a Theme

A *theme* is a collection of styles that override the look and feel of Android widgets. Themes were inspired by Cascading Style Sheets (CSS) used for web pages—they separate the content of a screen and its presentation or style. Android is packaged with several themes that you can reference by name,[4] or you can make up your own theme by subclassing existing ones and overriding their default values.

We could define our own custom theme in res/values/styles.xml, but for this example we'll just take advantage of a predefined one. To use it, open the AndroidManifest.xml editor again, and change the definition of the About activity so it has a theme property.

---

4. See http://code.google.com/android/reference/android/R.style.html for symbols beginning with "Theme_."

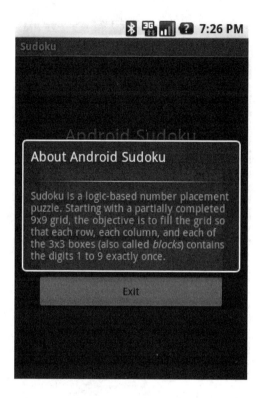

Figure 3.9: ABOUT SCREEN AFTER APPLYING THE DIALOG BOX THEME

Sudokuv1/AndroidManifest.xml

```
<activity android:name=".About"
     android:label="@string/about_title"
     android:theme="@android:style/Theme.Dialog">
</activity>
```

The @android: prefix in front of the style name means this is a reference to a resource defined by Android, not one that is defined in your program.

Running the program again, the About box now looks like Figure 3.9.

Many programs need menus and options, so the next two sections will show you how to define them.

3.7 Adding a Menu

Android supports two kinds of menus. First, there is the menu you get when you press the Menu button. Second, there is a context menu that

> ### Joe Asks...
> #### Why Not Use an HTML View?
>
> Android supports embedding a web browser directly into a view through the WebView class (see Section 7.2, *Web with a View*, on page 121). So, why didn't we just use that for the About box?
>
> Actually, you could do it either way. A WebView would support far more sophisticated formatting than a simple TextView, but it does have some limitations (such as the inability to use a transparent background). Also, WebView is a heavyweight widget that will be slower and take more memory than TextView. For your own applications, use whichever one makes the most sense for your needs.

pops up when you press and hold your finger on the screen (or press and hold the D-pad center button).

Let's do the first kind so that when the user presses the Menu key, they'll open a menu like the one in Figure 3.10, on the next page. First we need to define a few strings that we'll use later:

`Sudokuv1/res/values/strings.xml`

```
<string name="settings_label">Settings...</string>
<string name="settings_title">Sudoku settings</string>
<string name="settings_shortcut">s</string>
<string name="music_title">Music</string>
<string name="music_summary">Play background music</string>
<string name="hints_title">Hints</string>
<string name="hints_summary">Show hints during play</string>
```

Then we define the menu using XML in res/menu/menu.xml:

`Sudokuv1/res/menu/menu.xml`

```
<?xml version="1.0" encoding="utf-8"?>
<menu xmlns:android="http://schemas.android.com/apk/res/android">
    <item android:id="@+id/settings"
        android:title="@string/settings_label"
        android:alphabeticShortcut="@string/settings_shortcut" />
</menu>
```

Figure 3.10: PRESS THE MENU BUTTON TO OPEN THE MENU.

Next we need to modify the Sudoku class to bring up the menu we just defined. To do that, we'll need a few more imports:

Sudokuv1/src/org/example/sudoku/Sudoku.java

```java
import android.view.Menu;
import android.view.MenuInflater;
import android.view.MenuItem;
```

Then we override the Sudoku.onCreateOptionsMenu() method:

Sudokuv1/src/org/example/sudoku/Sudoku.java

```java
@Override
public boolean onCreateOptionsMenu(Menu menu) {
    super.onCreateOptionsMenu(menu);
    MenuInflater inflater = getMenuInflater();
    inflater.inflate(R.menu.menu, menu);
    return true;
}
```

getMenuInflater() returns an instance of MenuInflater that we use to read the menu definition from XML and turns it into a real view.

When the user selects any menu item, onOptionsItemSelected() will be called. Here's the definition for that method:

Sudokuv1/src/org/example/sudoku/Sudoku.java

```java
@Override
public boolean onOptionsItemSelected(MenuItem item) {
    switch (item.getItemId()) {
    case R.id.settings:
        startActivity(new Intent(this, Settings.class));
        return true;
    // More items go here (if any) ...
    }
    return false;
}
```

Settings is a class that we're going to define that displays all our preferences and allows the user to change them.

3.8 Adding Settings

Android provides a nice facility for defining what all your program preferences are and how to display them using almost no code. You define the preferences in a resource file called res/xml/settings.xml:

`Sudokuv1/res/xml/settings.xml`

```xml
<?xml version="1.0" encoding="utf-8"?>
<PreferenceScreen
    xmlns:android="http://schemas.android.com/apk/res/android">
    <CheckBoxPreference
        android:key="music"
        android:title="@string/music_title"
        android:summary="@string/music_summary"
        android:defaultValue="true" />
    <CheckBoxPreference
        android:key="hints"
        android:title="@string/hints_title"
        android:summary="@string/hints_summary"
        android:defaultValue="true" />
</PreferenceScreen>
```

The Sudoku program has two settings: one for background music and one for displaying hints. The keys are constant strings that will be used under the covers in Android's preferences database.

Next define the Settings class, and make it extend PreferenceActivity:

`Sudokuv1/src/org/example/sudoku/Settings.java`

```java
package org.example.sudoku;

import android.os.Bundle;
import android.preference.PreferenceActivity;

public class Settings extends PreferenceActivity {
    @Override
    protected void onCreate(Bundle savedInstanceState) {
        super.onCreate(savedInstanceState);
        addPreferencesFromResource(R.xml.settings);
    }
}
```

The addPreferencesFromResource() method reads the settings definition from XML and inflates it into views in the current activity. All the heavy lifting takes place in the PreferenceActivity class.

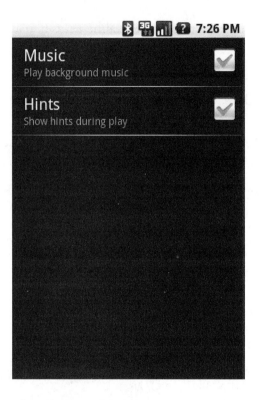

Figure 3.11: IT'S NOT MUCH TO LOOK AT, BUT WE GOT IT FOR FREE.

Don't forget to register the Settings activity in AndroidManifest.xml:

`Sudokuv1/AndroidManifest.xml`
```
<activity android:name=".Settings"
     android:label="@string/settings_title">
</activity>
```

Now rerun Sudoku, press the Menu key, select the Settings... item, and watch with amazement as the Sudoku settings page appears (see Figure 3.11). Try changing the values there and exiting the program, and then come back in and make sure they're all still set.

Code that reads the settings and does something with them will be discussed in a different chapter (Chapter 6, *Storing Local Data*, on page 105). For now let's move on to the New Game button.

3.9 Starting a New Game

If you've played any Sudoku games, you know that some are easy and some are maddeningly hard. So when the user selects New Game, we want to pop up a dialog box asking them to select between three difficulty levels. Selecting from a list of things is easy to do in Android. First we'll need a few more strings in res/values/strings.xml.

Sudokuv1/res/values/strings.xml

```
<string name="new_game_title">Difficulty</string>
<string name="easy_label">Easy</string>
<string name="medium_label">Medium</string>
<string name="hard_label">Hard</string>
```

Create the list of difficulties as an array resource in res/values/arrays.xml:

Sudokuv1/res/values/arrays.xml

```
<?xml version="1.0" encoding="utf-8"?>
<resources>
    <array name="difficulty">
        <item>@string/easy_label</item>
        <item>@string/medium_label</item>
        <item>@string/hard_label</item>
    </array>
</resources>
```

We'll need a few more imports in the Sudoku class:

Sudokuv1/src/org/example/sudoku/Sudoku.java

```
import android.app.AlertDialog;
import android.content.DialogInterface;
import android.util.Log;
```

Add code in the switch statement of the onClick() method to handle a click on the New Game button:

Sudokuv1/src/org/example/sudoku/Sudoku.java

```
case R.id.new_button:
    openNewGameDialog();
    break;
```

The openNewGameDialog() method takes care of creating the user interface for the difficulty list.

Figure 3.12: DIFFICULTY SELECTION DIALOG BOX

Sudokuv1/src/org/example/sudoku/Sudoku.java

```java
private static final String TAG = "Sudoku";

/** Ask the user what difficulty level they want */
private void openNewGameDialog() {
    new AlertDialog.Builder(this)
        .setTitle(R.string.new_game_title)
        .setItems(R.array.difficulty,
         new DialogInterface.OnClickListener() {
            public void onClick(DialogInterface dialoginterface,
                    int i) {
                startGame(i);
            }
        })
        .show();
}

/** Start a new game with the given difficulty level */
private void startGame(int i) {
    Log.d(TAG, "clicked on " + i);
    // Start game here...
}
```

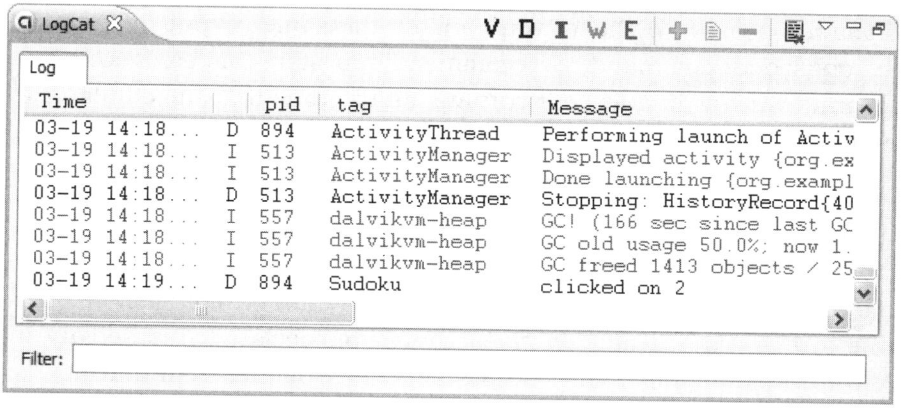

Figure 3.13: DEBUGGING OUTPUT IN THE LOGCAT VIEW

The setItems() method takes two parameters: the resource ID of the item list and a listener that will be called when one of the items is selected.

When you run the program now and press New Game, you'll get the dialog box in Figure 3.12, on the facing page.

We're not actually going to start the game yet, so instead when you select a difficulty level, we just print a debug message using the Log.d() method, passing it a tag string and a message to print.

3.10 Debugging with Log Messages

The Log class provides several static methods to print messages of various severity levels to the Android system log:

- Log.e(): Errors
- Log.w(): Warnings
- Log.i(): Information
- Log.d(): Debugging
- Log.v(): Verbose

Users will never see this log, but as a developer you can view it in a couple ways. In Eclipse, open the LogCat view by selecting Window > Show View > Other... > Android > LogCat (see Figure 3.13). The view can be filtered by severity or by the tag you specified on the method call.

If you're not using Eclipse, you can see the same output by running the `adb logcat` command.[5] I recommend you start this command in a separate window and leave it running all the time that the emulator is running. It won't interfere with any other monitors.

I can't stress enough how useful the Android log will be during development. Remember that error we saw earlier with the About box (Figure 3.7, on page 44)? If you had opened the LogCat view at that point, you would have seen this message: "ActivityNotFoundException: Unable to find explicit activity class...have you declared this activity in your AndroidManifest.xml?" It doesn't get any plainer than that.

3.11 Debugging with the Debugger

In addition to log messages, you can use the Eclipse debugger to set breakpoints, single step, and view the state of your program. First, enable your project for debugging by adding the `android:debuggable="true"` option in your AndroidManifest.xml file:[6]

`Sudokuv1/AndroidManifest.xml`

```
<application android:icon="@drawable/icon"
      android:label="@string/app_name"
      android:debuggable="true">
```

Then, simply right-click the project, and select Debug As > Android Application.

3.12 Exiting the Game

This game doesn't really need an Exit button, because the user can just press the Back key or the Home key to do something else. But I wanted to add one to show you how to terminate an activity. Add this to the switch statement in the onClick() method:

`Sudokuv1/src/org/example/sudoku/Sudoku.java`

```
case R.id.exit_button:
   finish();
   break;
```

---

5. http://code.google.com/android/reference/adb.html
6. This is optional if you're using the emulator but required on a real device. Just remember to remove the option before releasing your code to the public.

When the Exit button is selected, we call the finish() method. This shuts down the activity and returns control to the next activity on the Android application stack (usually the Home screen).

3.13 Fast-Forward >>

Whew, that was a lot to cover in one chapter! Starting from scratch, you learned how to use layout files to organize your user interface and how to use Android resources for text, colors, and more. You added controls such as buttons and text fields, applied themes to change the program's appearance, and even added menus and preferences for good measure.

Android is a complex system, but you don't have to know all of it to get started. When you need help, the hundreds of pages of reference material online go into more depth on all the classes and methods used here.[7]

In Chapter 4, *Exploring 2D Graphics*, on page 57, we'll use Android's graphics API to draw the tiles for the Sudoku game.

---

7. To view the online documentation, open documentation.html from your Android SDK install location, or point your browser to http://code.google.com/android/documentation.html.

Exploring 2D Graphics

So far, we've covered the basic concepts and philosophy of Android and how to create a simple user interface with a few buttons and a dialog box. You're really starting to get the hang of this Android thing. But something is missing...what is it? Oh yeah, the fun!

Good graphics can add a bit of fun and excitement to any application. Android puts one of the most powerful graphics libraries available on a mobile device at your fingertips. Actually, it puts two of them there: one for two-dimensional graphics and one for three-dimensional graphics.[1]

In this chapter, we will cover 2D graphics and apply that knowledge to implement the game part of our Sudoku example. Chapter 10, *3D Graphics in OpenGL*, on page 181 will cover 3D graphics using the OpenGL ES library.

4.1 Learning the Basics

Android provides a complete native two-dimensional graphics library in its android.graphics package. With a basic understanding of classes such as Color and Canvas, you'll be up and drawing in no time.

Color

Android colors are represented with four numbers, one each for alpha, red, green, and blue (ARGB). Each component can have 256 possible values, or 8 bits, so a color is typically packed into a 32-bit integer. For

---

1. Functionality for four-dimensional graphics was considered for Android, but it was dropped because of a lack of time.

efficiency, Android code uses an integer instead of an instance of the Color class.

Red, green, and blue are self-explanatory, but alpha might not be. *Alpha* is a measure of transparency. The lowest value, 0, indicates the color is completely transparent. It doesn't really matter what the values for RGB are, if A is 0. The highest value, 255, indicates the color is completely opaque. Values in the middle are used for translucent, or semitransparent, colors. They let you see some of what is underneath the object being drawn in the foreground.

To create a color, you can use one of the static constants on the Color class, like this:

```
int color = Color.BLUE; // solid blue
```

or if you know the alpha, red, green, and blue numbers, you can use one of the static factory methods such as the following:

```
// Translucent purple
color = Color.argb(127, 255, 0, 255);
```

If possible, though, you're usually better off defining all your colors in an XML resource file. This lets you change them easily in one place later:

```
<?xml version="1.0" encoding="utf-8"?>
<resources>
   <color name="mycolor">#7fff00ff</color>
</resources>
```

You can reference colors by name in other XML files, as we did in Chapter 3, or you can use them in Java code like this:

```
color = getResources().getColor(R.color.mycolor);
```

The getResources() method returns the ResourceManager class for the current activity, and getColor() asks the manager to look up a color given a resource ID.

Paint

One of the Android native graphics library's most important classes is the Paint class. It holds the style, color, and other information needed to draw any graphics including bitmaps, text, and geometric shapes.

Normally when you paint something on the screen, you want to draw it in a solid color. You set that color with the Paint.setColor() method.

For example:

```
cPaint.setColor(Color.LTGRAY);
```

This uses the predefined color value for light gray.

Canvas

The Canvas class represents a surface on which you draw. Initially canvases start off devoid of any content, like blank transparencies for an overhead projector. Methods on the Canvas class let you draw lines, rectangles, circles, or other arbitrary graphics on the surface.

In Android, the display screen is taken up by an Activity, which hosts a View, which in turn hosts a Canvas. You get an opportunity to draw on that canvas by overriding the View.onDraw() method. The only parameter to onDraw() is a canvas on which you can draw.

Here's an example activity called Graphics, which contains a view called GraphicsView:

```
public class Graphics extends Activity {
    @Override
    public void onCreate(Bundle savedInstanceState) {
        super.onCreate(savedInstanceState);
        setContentView(new GraphicsView(this));
    }

    static public class GraphicsView extends View {
        public GraphicsView(Context context) {
            super(context);
        }
        @Override
        protected void onDraw(Canvas canvas) {
            // Drawing commands go here
        }
    }
}
```

We're going to put some drawing commands into the onDraw() method in the next section.

Path

The Path class holds a set of vector-drawing commands such as lines, rectangles, and curves. Here's an example that defines a circular path:

```
circle = new Path();
circle.addCircle(150, 150, 100, Direction.CW);
```

Graphics

Figure 4.1: DRAWING TEXT AROUND A CIRCLE

This defines a circle at position x=150, y=150, with a radius of 100 pixels. Now that we've defined the path, let's use it to draw the circle's outline plus some text around the inside:

```
private static final String QUOTE = "Now is the time for all " +
        "good men to come to the aid of their country.";
    canvas.drawPath(circle, cPaint);
    canvas.drawTextOnPath(QUOTE, circle, 0, 20, tPaint);
```

You can see the result in Figure 4.1. Since the circle was drawn in the clockwise direction (Direction.CW), the text is also drawn that way.

If you want to get really fancy, Android provides a number of PathEffect classes that let you do things such as apply a random permutation to a path, cause all the line segments along a path to be smoothed out with curves or broken up into segments, and create other effects.

Drawable

In Android, a Drawable class is used for a visual element like a bitmap or solid color that is intended for display only. You can combine drawables with other graphics, or you can use them in user interface widgets (for example, as the background for a button or view).

Drawables can take a variety of forms:

- *Bitmap*: A PNG or JPEG image.
- *NinePatch*: A stretchable PNG image, so named because originally it divided the image into nine sections. These are used for the background of resizable bitmap buttons.
- *Shape*: Vector-drawing commands, based on Path. This is sort of a poor man's SVG.
- *Layers*: A container for child drawables that draw on top of each other in a certain z-order.
- *States*: A container that shows one of its child drawables based on its state (a bit mask). One use is to set various selection and focus states for buttons.
- *Levels*: A container that shows only one of its child drawables based on its level (a range of integers). This could be used for a battery or signal strength gauge.
- *Scale*: A container for one child drawable that modifies its size based on the current level. One use might be a zoomable picture viewer.

Drawables are almost always defined in XML. Here's a common example where a drawable is defined to be a gradient from one color to another (in this case, white to gray). The angle specifies the direction of the gradient (270 degrees means top to bottom). This will be used for the background of a view:

```
<?xml version="1.0" encoding="utf-8"?>
<shape xmlns:android="http://schemas.android.com/apk/res/android">
   <gradient
       android:startColor="#FFFFFF"
       android:endColor="#808080"
       android:angle="270" />
</shape>
```

To use it, we could either refer to it in XML with the android:background= attribute or call the Canvas.setBackgroundResource() method in the view's onCreate() method like this:

```
setBackgroundResource(R.drawable.background);
```

This gives our GraphicsView example a nice gradient background, as shown in Figure 4.2, on the following page.

Figure 4.2: USING A GRADIENT BACKGROUND DEFINED IN XML

4.2 Adding Graphics to Sudoku

It's time to apply what we've learned to our Sudoku example. When we left it at the end of Chapter 3, the Sudoku game had an opening screen, an About dialog box, and a way to start a new game. But it was missing one very important part: the game! We'll use the native 2D graphics library to implement that part.

Starting the Game

First we need to fill in the code that starts the game. startGame() takes one parameter, the index of the difficulty name selected from the list. Here's its definition:

```
Sudokuv2/src/org/example/sudoku/Sudoku.java
/** Start a new game with the given difficulty level */
private void startGame(int i) {
    Log.d(TAG, "clicked on " + i);
    Intent intent = new Intent(Sudoku.this, Game.class);
    intent.putExtra(Game.KEY_DIFFICULTY, i);
    startActivity(intent);
}
```

> ### Sudoku Trivia
>
> A few years after it was published in the United States, Number Place was picked up by the Japanese publisher Nikoli, who gave it the much cooler-sounding name Sudoku (which means "single number" in Japanese). From there it was exported around the world, and the rest is history. Sadly, Garns died in 1989 before getting a chance to see his creation become a worldwide sensation.

The game part of Sudoku will be another activity called Game, so we create a new intent to kick it off. We place the difficulty number in an extraData area provided in the intent, and then we call the startActivity() method to launch the new activity.

The extraData area is a map of key/value pairs that will be passed along to the intent. The keys are strings, and the values can be any primitive type, array of primitives, Bundle, or a subclass of Serializable or Parcelable. In a real program, you may want to prefix the key names with the name of your package.

Defining the Game Class

Here's the outline of the Game activity:

Sudokuv2/src/org/example/sudoku/Game.java

```java
package org.example.sudoku;

import android.app.Activity;
import android.app.Dialog;
import android.os.Bundle;
import android.util.Log;
import android.view.Gravity;
import android.widget.Toast;

public class Game extends Activity {
    private static final String TAG = "Sudoku";

    public static final String KEY_DIFFICULTY = "difficulty";
    public static final int DIFFICULTY_EASY = 0;
    public static final int DIFFICULTY_MEDIUM = 1;
    public static final int DIFFICULTY_HARD = 2;

    private int puzzle[] = new int[9 * 9];

    private PuzzleView puzzleView;
```

```
@Override
protected void onCreate(Bundle savedInstanceState) {
    super.onCreate(savedInstanceState);
    Log.d(TAG, "onCreate");

    int diff = getIntent().getIntExtra(KEY_DIFFICULTY,
            DIFFICULTY_EASY);
    puzzle = getPuzzle(diff);
    calculateUsedTiles();

    puzzleView = new PuzzleView(this);
    setContentView(puzzleView);
    puzzleView.requestFocus();
}
// ...
}
```

The onCreate() method fetches the difficulty number from the intent and selects a puzzle to play. Then it creates an instance of the PuzzleView class, setting the PuzzleView as the new contents of the view. Since this is a fully customized view, it was easier to do this in code than in XML.

The calculateUsedTiles() method, which is not shown here, uses the rules of Sudoku to figure out, for each tile in the nine-by-nine grid, which numbers are not valid for the tile because they appear elsewhere in the horizontal or vertical direction or in the three-by-three subgrid.

This is an activity, so we need to register it in AndroidManifest.xml:

Sudokuv2/AndroidManifest.xml

```xml
<activity android:name=".Game"
        android:label="@string/game_title"/>
```

We also need to add a few more string resources to res/values/strings.xml:

Sudokuv2/res/values/strings.xml

```xml
<string name="game_title">Game</string>
<string name="no_moves_label">No moves</string>
<string name="keypad_title">Keypad</string>
```

Defining the PuzzleView Class

Next we need to define the PuzzleView class. Instead of using an XML layout, this time let's do it entirely in Java.

> ### What Size Is It Anyway?
>
> A common mistake made by new Android developers is to use the width and height of a view inside its constructor. When a view's constructor is called, Android doesn't know yet how big the view will be, so the sizes are set to zero. The real sizes are calculated during the layout stage, which occurs after construction but before anything is drawn. You can use the onSizeChanged() method to be notified of the values when they are known, or you can use the getWidth() and getHeight() methods later, such as in the onDraw() method.

Here's the outline:

Sudokuv2/src/org/example/sudoku/PuzzleView.java

```java
package org.example.sudoku;

import android.content.Context;
import android.graphics.Canvas;
import android.graphics.Paint;
import android.graphics.Rect;
import android.graphics.Paint.FontMetrics;
import android.graphics.Paint.Style;
import android.util.Log;
import android.view.KeyEvent;
import android.view.MotionEvent;
import android.view.View;
import android.view.animation.AnimationUtils;

public class PuzzleView extends View {
    private static final String TAG = "Sudoku";
    private final Game game;
    public PuzzleView(Context context) {
        super(context);
        this.game = (Game) context;
        setFocusable(true);
        setFocusableInTouchMode(true);
    }
    // ...
}
```

In the constructor we keep a reference to the Game class and set the option to allow user input in the view. Inside PuzzleView, we need to implement the onSizeChanged() method. This is called after the view is created and Android knows how big everything is.

```
Sudokuv2/src/org/example/sudoku/PuzzleView.java
private float width;      // width of one tile
private float height;     // height of one tile
private int selX;         // X index of selection
private int selY;         // Y index of selection
private final Rect selRect = new Rect();

@Override
protected void onSizeChanged(int w, int h, int oldw, int oldh) {
    width = w / 9f;
    height = h / 9f;
    getRect(selX, selY, selRect);
    Log.d(TAG, "onSizeChanged: width " + width + ", height "
        + height);
    super.onSizeChanged(w, h, oldw, oldh);
}
```

We use onSizeChanged() to calculate the size of each tile on the screen (1/9th of the total view width and height). Note this is a floating-point number, so it's possible that we could end up with a fractional number of pixels. selRect is a rectangle we'll use later to keep track of the selection cursor.

At this point we've created a view for the puzzle, and we know how big it is. The next step is to draw the grid lines that separate the tiles on the board.

Drawing the Board

Android calls a view's onDraw() method every time any part of the view needs to be updated. To simplify things, onDraw() pretends that you're re-creating the entire screen from scratch. In reality, you may be drawing only a small portion of the view as defined by the canvas's clip rectangle. Android takes care of doing the clipping for you.

Start by defining a few new colors to play with in res/values/colors.xml:

```
Sudokuv2/res/values/colors.xml
<color name="puzzle_background">#ffe6f0ff</color>
<color name="puzzle_hilite">#ffffffff</color>
<color name="puzzle_light">#64c6d4ef</color>
<color name="puzzle_dark">#6456648f</color>
<color name="puzzle_foreground">#ff000000</color>
<color name="puzzle_hint_0">#64ff0000</color>
<color name="puzzle_hint_1">#6400ff80</color>
<color name="puzzle_hint_2">#2000ff80</color>
<color name="puzzle_selected">#64ff8000</color>
```

> **Other Ways to Do It**
>
> When I was writing this example, I tried several different approaches such as using a button for each tile or declaring a grid of ImageView classes in XML. After many false starts, I found that the approach of having one view for the entire puzzle and drawing lines and numbers inside that proved to be the fastest and easiest way for this application.
>
> It does have its drawbacks, though, such as the need to draw the selection and explicitly handle keyboard and touch events. When designing your own program, I recommend trying standard widgets and views first and then falling back to custom drawing only if that doesn't work for you.

Here's the basic outline for onDraw():

Sudokuv2/src/org/example/sudoku/PuzzleView.java

```java
@Override
protected void onDraw(Canvas canvas) {
    // Draw the background...
    Paint background = new Paint();
    background.setColor(getResources().getColor(
        R.color.puzzle_background));
    canvas.drawRect(0, 0, getWidth(), getHeight(), background);

    // Draw the board...
    // Draw the numbers...
    // Draw the hints...
    // Draw the selection...
}
```

The first parameter is the Canvas on which to draw. In this code, we're just drawing a background for the puzzle using the puzzle_background color.

Now let's add the code to draw the grid lines for the board:

Sudokuv2/src/org/example/sudoku/PuzzleView.java

```java
// Draw the board...
// Define colors for the grid lines
Paint dark = new Paint();
dark.setColor(getResources().getColor(R.color.puzzle_dark));

Paint hilite = new Paint();
hilite.setColor(getResources().getColor(R.color.puzzle_hilite));
```

```
Paint light = new Paint();
light.setColor(getResources().getColor(R.color.puzzle_light));

// Draw the minor grid lines
for (int i = 0; i < 9; i++) {
   canvas.drawLine(0, i * height, getWidth(), i * height,
         light);
   canvas.drawLine(0, i * height + 1, getWidth(), i * height
         + 1, hilite);
   canvas.drawLine(i * width, 0, i * width, getHeight(),
         light);
   canvas.drawLine(i * width + 1, 0, i * width + 1,
         getHeight(), hilite);
}

// Draw the major grid lines
for (int i = 0; i < 9; i++) {
   if (i % 3 != 0)
      continue;
   canvas.drawLine(0, i * height, getWidth(), i * height,
         dark);
   canvas.drawLine(0, i * height + 1, getWidth(), i * height
         + 1, hilite);
   canvas.drawLine(i * width, 0, i * width, getHeight(), dark);
   canvas.drawLine(i * width + 1, 0, i * width + 1,
         getHeight(), hilite);
}
```

The code uses three different colors for the grid lines: a light color between each tile, a dark color between the three-by-three blocks, and a highlight color drawn on the edge of each tile to make them look like they have a little depth. The order in which the lines are drawn is important, since lines drawn later will be drawn over the top of earlier lines. You can see what this will look like in Figure 4.3, on the next page. Next, we need some numbers to go inside those lines.

Drawing the Numbers

The following code draws the puzzle numbers on top of the tiles. The tricky part here is getting each number positioned and sized so it goes in the exact center of its tile.

Sudokuv2/src/org/example/sudoku/PuzzleView.java

```
// Draw the numbers...
// Define color and style for numbers
Paint foreground = new Paint(Paint.ANTI_ALIAS_FLAG);
foreground.setColor(getResources().getColor(
      R.color.puzzle_foreground));
foreground.setStyle(Style.FILL);
```

Figure 4.3: Drawing the grid lines with three colors for effect

```
foreground.setTextSize(height * 0.75f);
foreground.setTextScaleX(width / height);
foreground.setTextAlign(Paint.Align.CENTER);

// Draw the number in the center of the tile
FontMetrics fm = foreground.getFontMetrics();
// Centering in X: use alignment (and X at midpoint)
float x = width / 2;
// Centering in Y: measure ascent/descent first
float y = height / 2 - (fm.ascent + fm.descent) / 2;
for (int i = 0; i < 9; i++) {
   for (int j = 0; j < 9; j++) {
      canvas.drawText(this.game.getTileString(i, j), i
            * width + x, j * height + y, foreground);
   }
}
```

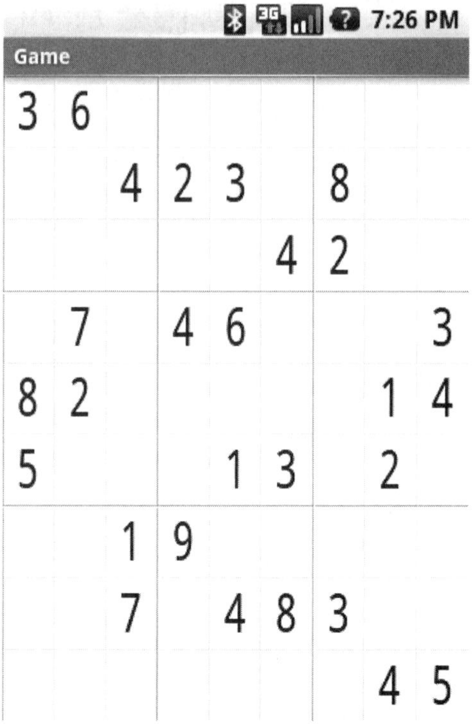

Figure 4.4: CENTERING THE NUMBERS INSIDE THE TILES

To calculate the size of the numbers, we set the font height to three-fourths the height of the tile, and we set the aspect ratio to be the same as the tile's aspect ratio. We can't use absolute pixel or point sizes because we want the program to work at any resolution.

To determine the position of each number, we center it in both the x and y dimensions. The x direction is easy—just divide the tile width by 2. But for the y direction, we have to adjust the starting position downward a little so that the midpoint of the tile will be the midpoint of the number instead of its baseline. We use the graphics library's FontMetrics class to tell how much vertical space the letter will take in total, and then we divide that in half to get the adjustment. You can see the results in Figure 4.4.

That takes care of displaying the puzzle's starting numbers (the givens). The next step is to allow the player to enter their guesses for all the blank spaces.

Figure 4.5: DRAWING AND MOVING THE SELECTION

4.3 Handling Input

One difference in Android programming—as opposed to, say, iPhone programming—is that Android phones come in many shapes and sizes and have a variety of input methods. They might have a keyboard, a D-pad, a touch screen, a trackball, or some combination of these.

A good Android program, therefore, needs to be ready to support whatever input hardware is available, just like it needs to be ready to support any screen resolution.

Defining and Updating the Selection

First we're going to implement a little cursor that shows the player which tile is currently selected. The selected tile is the one that will be modified when the player enters a number. This code will draw the selection in onDraw():

`Sudokuv2/src/org/example/sudoku/PuzzleView.java`

```
// Draw the selection...
Log.d(TAG, "selRect=" + selRect);
Paint selected = new Paint();
selected.setColor(getResources().getColor(
      R.color.puzzle_selected));
canvas.drawRect(selRect, selected);
```

We use the selection rectangle calculated earlier in onSizeChanged() to draw an alpha-blended color on top of the selected tile.

Next we provide a way to move the selection by overriding the onKey-Down() method:

```
Sudokuv2/src/org/example/sudoku/PuzzleView.java
@Override
public boolean onKeyDown(int keyCode, KeyEvent event) {
   Log.d(TAG, "onKeyDown: keycode=" + keyCode + ", event="
         + event);
   switch (keyCode) {
   case KeyEvent.KEYCODE_DPAD_UP:
      select(selX, selY - 1);
      break;
   case KeyEvent.KEYCODE_DPAD_DOWN:
      select(selX, selY + 1);
      break;
   case KeyEvent.KEYCODE_DPAD_LEFT:
      select(selX - 1, selY);
      break;
   case KeyEvent.KEYCODE_DPAD_RIGHT:
      select(selX + 1, selY);
      break;
   default:
      return super.onKeyDown(keyCode, event);
   }
   return true;
}
```

If the user has a directional pad (D-pad) and they press the up, down, left, or right button, we call select() to move the selection cursor in that direction.

How about a trackball? We could override the onTrackballEvent() method, but it turns out that if you don't handle trackball events, Android will translate them into D-pad events automatically. Therefore, we can leave it out for this example.

Inside the select() method, we calculate the new x and y coordinate of the selection and then use getRect() again to calculate the new selection rectangle:

```
Sudokuv2/src/org/example/sudoku/PuzzleView.java
private void select(int x, int y) {
   invalidate(selRect);
   selX = Math.min(Math.max(x, 0), 8);
   selY = Math.min(Math.max(y, 0), 8);
   getRect(selX, selY, selRect);
   invalidate(selRect);
}
```

```
private void getRect(int x, int y, Rect rect) {
   rect.set((int) (x * width), (int) (y * height), (int) (x
         * width + width), (int) (y * height + height));
}
```

Notice the two calls to invalidate(). The first one tells Android that the area covered by the old selection rectangle (on the left of Figure 4.5, on page 71) needs to be redrawn. The second invalidate() call says that the new selection area (on the right of the figure) needs to be redrawn too. We don't actually draw anything here.

This is an important point: never call any drawing functions except in the onDraw() method. Instead, you use the invalidate() method to mark rectangles as *dirty*. The window manager will combine all the dirty rectangles at some point in the future and call onDraw() again for you. The dirty rectangles become the clip region, so screen updates are optimized to only those areas that change.

Now let's provide a way for the player to enter a new number on the selected tile.

Entering Numbers

To handle keyboard input, we just add a few more cases to the onKey-Down() method for the numbers 0 through 9 (0 or space means erase the number).

Sudokuv2/src/org/example/sudoku/PuzzleView.java
```
case KeyEvent.KEYCODE_0:
case KeyEvent.KEYCODE_SPACE: setSelectedTile(0); break;
case KeyEvent.KEYCODE_1:      setSelectedTile(1); break;
case KeyEvent.KEYCODE_2:      setSelectedTile(2); break;
case KeyEvent.KEYCODE_3:      setSelectedTile(3); break;
case KeyEvent.KEYCODE_4:      setSelectedTile(4); break;
case KeyEvent.KEYCODE_5:      setSelectedTile(5); break;
case KeyEvent.KEYCODE_6:      setSelectedTile(6); break;
case KeyEvent.KEYCODE_7:      setSelectedTile(7); break;
case KeyEvent.KEYCODE_8:      setSelectedTile(8); break;
case KeyEvent.KEYCODE_9:      setSelectedTile(9); break;
case KeyEvent.KEYCODE_ENTER:
case KeyEvent.KEYCODE_DPAD_CENTER:
   game.showKeypadOrError(selX, selY);
   break;
```

To support the D-pad, we check for the Enter or center D-pad button in onKeyDown() and have it pop up a keypad that lets the user select which number to place.

Optimizing Refreshes

In an earlier version of this example, I invalidated the entire screen whenever the cursor was moved. Thus, on every key press, the whole puzzle had to be redrawn. This caused it to lag noticeably. Switching the code to invalidate only the smallest rectangles that changed made it run much faster.

For touch, we override the onTouchEvent() method and show the same keypad, which will be defined later:

Sudokuv2/src/org/example/sudoku/PuzzleView.java

```
@Override
public boolean onTouchEvent(MotionEvent event) {
    if (event.getAction() != MotionEvent.ACTION_DOWN)
        return super.onTouchEvent(event);

    select((int) (event.getX() / width),
        (int) (event.getY() / height));
    game.showKeypadOrError(selX, selY);
    Log.d(TAG, "onTouchEvent: x " + selX + ", y " + selY);
    return true;
}
```

Ultimately, all roads will lead back to a call to setSelectedTile() to change the number on a tile:

Sudokuv2/src/org/example/sudoku/PuzzleView.java

```
public void setSelectedTile(int tile) {
    if (game.setTileIfValid(selX, selY, tile)) {
        invalidate();// may change hints
    } else {
        // Number is not valid for this tile
        Log.d(TAG, "setSelectedTile: invalid: " + tile);
    }
}
```

Note the call to invalidate() with no parameters. That marks the whole screen as dirty, which violates my own advice earlier! However, in this case, it's necessary because any new numbers added or removed might change the hints that we are about to implement in the next section.

Adding Hints

How can we help the player out a little without solving the whole puzzle for them? How about if we draw the background of each tile differently depending on how many possible moves it has. Add this to onDraw() before drawing the selection:

```
// Draw the hints...
// Pick a hint color based on #moves left
Paint hint = new Paint();
int c[] = { getResources().getColor(R.color.puzzle_hint_0),
      getResources().getColor(R.color.puzzle_hint_1),
      getResources().getColor(R.color.puzzle_hint_2), };
Rect r = new Rect();
for (int i = 0; i < 9; i++) {
   for (int j = 0; j < 9; j++) {
      int movesleft = 9 - game.getUsedTiles(i, j).length;
      if (movesleft < c.length) {
         getRect(i, j, r);
         hint.setColor(c[movesleft]);
         canvas.drawRect(r, hint);
      }
   }
}
```

We use three states for zero, one, and two possible moves. If there are zero moves, that means the player has done something wrong and needs to backtrack.

The result will look like Figure 4.6, on the following page. Can you spot the mistake(s) made by the player?[2]

Shaking Things Up

What if the user tries to enter an obviously invalid number, such as a number that already appears in the three-by-three block? Just for fun, let's make the screen wiggle back and forth when they do that. First we add a call to the invalid number case in setSelectedTile():

```
// Number is not valid for this tile
Log.d(TAG, "setSelectedTile: invalid: " + tile);
startAnimation(AnimationUtils.loadAnimation(game,
      R.anim.shake));
```

---

2. The two numbers on the bottom row, middle block, are wrong.

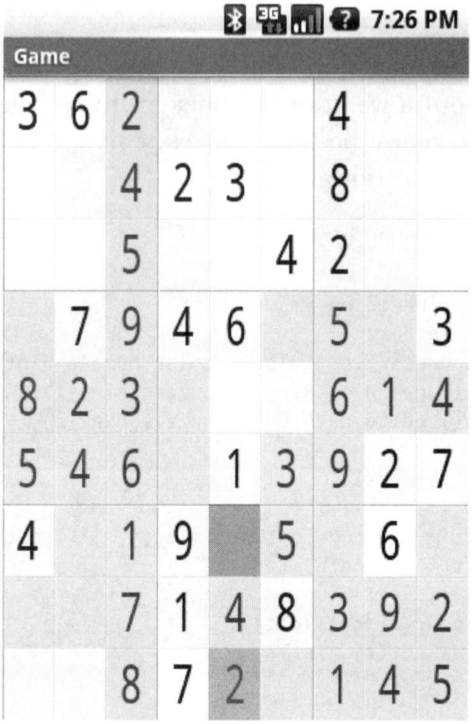

Figure 4.6: Tiles are highlighted based on how many possible values the tile can have.

This loads and runs a resource called R.anim.shake, defined in res/anim/shake.xml, that shakes the screen for 1,000 milliseconds (1 second) by 10 pixels from side to side.

Sudokuv2/res/anim/shake.xml

```xml
<?xml version="1.0" encoding="utf-8"?>
<translate
    xmlns:android="http://schemas.android.com/apk/res/android"
    android:fromXDelta="0"
    android:toXDelta="10"
    android:duration="1000"
    android:interpolator="@anim/cycle_7" />
```

The number of times to run the animation and the velocity and acceleration of the animation are controlled by an animation interpolator defined in XML.

```
Sudokuv2/res/anim/cycle_7.xml
```

```xml
<?xml version="1.0" encoding="utf-8"?>
<cycleInterpolator
    xmlns:android="http://schemas.android.com/apk/res/android"
    android:cycles="7" />
```

This particular one will cause the animation to be repeated seven times.

4.4 The Rest of the Story

Now let's go back and tie up a few loose ends, starting with the Keypad class. These pieces are necessary for the program to compile and operate but have nothing to do with graphics. Feel free to skip ahead to Section 4.5, *Making More Improvements*, on page 86 if you like.

Creating the Keypad

The keypad is handy for phones that don't have keyboards. It displays a grid of the numbers 1 through 9 in an activity that appears on top of the puzzle. The whole purpose of the keypad dialog box is to return a number selected by the player.

Here's the user interface layout from res/layout/keypad.xml:

```
Sudokuv2/res/layout/keypad.xml
```

```xml
<?xml version="1.0" encoding="utf-8"?>
<TableLayout
    xmlns:android="http://schemas.android.com/apk/res/android"
    android:id="@+id/keypad"
    android:orientation="vertical"
    android:layout_width="wrap_content"
    android:layout_height="wrap_content"
    android:stretchColumns="*">
    <TableRow>
        <Button android:id="@+id/keypad_1"
            android:text="1">
        </Button>
        <Button android:id="@+id/keypad_2"
            android:text="2">
        </Button>
        <Button android:id="@+id/keypad_3"
            android:text="3">
        </Button>
    </TableRow>
    <TableRow>
        <Button android:id="@+id/keypad_4"
            android:text="4">
        </Button>
```

```
        <Button android:id="@+id/keypad_5"
           android:text="5">
        </Button>
        <Button android:id="@+id/keypad_6"
           android:text="6">
        </Button>
     </TableRow>
     <TableRow>
        <Button android:id="@+id/keypad_7"
           android:text="7">
        </Button>
        <Button android:id="@+id/keypad_8"
           android:text="8">
        </Button>
        <Button android:id="@+id/keypad_9"
           android:text="9">
        </Button>
     </TableRow>
</TableLayout>
```

Next let's define the Keypad class. Here's the outline:

Sudokuv2/src/org/example/sudoku/Keypad.java

```java
package org.example.sudoku;

import android.app.Dialog;
import android.content.Context;
import android.os.Bundle;
import android.view.KeyEvent;
import android.view.View;

public class Keypad extends Dialog {

   protected static final String TAG = "Sudoku";

   private final View keys[] = new View[9];
   private View keypad;

   private final int useds[];
   private final PuzzleView puzzleView;

   public Keypad(Context context, int useds[], PuzzleView puzzleView) {
      super(context);
      this.useds = useds;
      this.puzzleView = puzzleView;
   }

   @Override
   protected void onCreate(Bundle savedInstanceState) {
      super.onCreate(savedInstanceState);
```

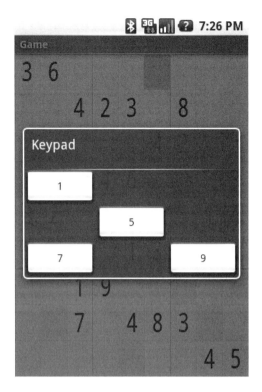

Figure 4.7: INVALID VALUES ARE HIDDEN IN THE KEYPAD VIEW.

```
    setContentView(R.layout.keypad);
    findViews();
    for (int element : useds) {
      if (element != 0)
        keys[element - 1].setVisibility(View.INVISIBLE);
    }
    setListeners();
  }

  // ...
}
```

If a particular number is not valid (for example, the same number already appears in that row), then we make the number invisible in the grid so the player can't select it (see Figure 4.7).

The findViews() method fetches and saves the views for all the keypad keys and the main keypad window:

```java
private void findViews() {
    keypad = findViewById(R.id.keypad);
    keys[0] = findViewById(R.id.keypad_1);
    keys[1] = findViewById(R.id.keypad_2);
    keys[2] = findViewById(R.id.keypad_3);
    keys[3] = findViewById(R.id.keypad_4);
    keys[4] = findViewById(R.id.keypad_5);
    keys[5] = findViewById(R.id.keypad_6);
    keys[6] = findViewById(R.id.keypad_7);
    keys[7] = findViewById(R.id.keypad_8);
    keys[8] = findViewById(R.id.keypad_9);
}
```

setListeners() loops through all the keypad keys and sets a listener for each one. It also sets a listener for the main keypad window:

```java
private void setListeners() {
    for (int i = 0; i < keys.length; i++) {
        final int t = i + 1;
        keys[i].setOnClickListener(new View.OnClickListener(){
            public void onClick(View v) {
                returnResult(t);
            }});
    }
    keypad.setOnClickListener(new View.OnClickListener(){
        public void onClick(View v) {
            returnResult(0);
        }});
}
```

When the player selects one of the buttons on the keypad, it calls the returnResult() method with the number for that button. If the player selects a place that doesn't have a button, then returnResult() is called with a zero, indicating the tile should be erased.

onKeyDown() is called when the player uses the keyboard to enter a number:

```java
@Override
public boolean onKeyDown(int keyCode, KeyEvent event) {
    int tile = 0;
    switch (keyCode) {
    case KeyEvent.KEYCODE_0:
    case KeyEvent.KEYCODE_SPACE: tile = 0; break;
```

```
case KeyEvent.KEYCODE_1:    tile = 1; break;
case KeyEvent.KEYCODE_2:    tile = 2; break;
case KeyEvent.KEYCODE_3:    tile = 3; break;
case KeyEvent.KEYCODE_4:    tile = 4; break;
case KeyEvent.KEYCODE_5:    tile = 5; break;
case KeyEvent.KEYCODE_6:    tile = 6; break;
case KeyEvent.KEYCODE_7:    tile = 7; break;
case KeyEvent.KEYCODE_8:    tile = 8; break;
case KeyEvent.KEYCODE_9:    tile = 9; break;
default:
    return super.onKeyDown(keyCode, event);
}
if (isValid(tile)) {
    returnResult(tile);
}
return true;

}
```

If the number is valid for the current tile, then it calls returnResult();
otherwise, the keystroke is ignored.

The isValid() method checks to see whether the given number is valid for
the current position:

Sudokuv2/src/org/example/sudoku/Keypad.java

```
private boolean isValid(int tile) {
    for (int t : useds) {
        if (tile == t)
            return false;
    }
    return true;
}
```

If it appears in the used array, then it's not valid because the same
number is already used in the current row, column, or block.

The returnResult() method is called to return the number selected to the
calling activity:

Sudokuv2/src/org/example/sudoku/Keypad.java

```
/** Return the chosen tile to the caller */
private void returnResult(int tile) {
    puzzleView.setSelectedTile(tile);
    dismiss();
}
```

We call the PuzzleView.setSelectedTile method to change the puzzle's current tile. The dismiss call terminates the Keypad dialog box.

Now that we have the activity, let's call it in the Game class and retrieve the result:

```
Sudokuv2/src/org/example/sudoku/Game.java
/** Open the keypad if there are any valid moves */
protected void showKeypadOrError(int x, int y) {
    int tiles[] = getUsedTiles(x, y);
    if (tiles.length == 9) {
        Toast toast = Toast.makeText(this,
                R.string.no_moves_label, Toast.LENGTH_SHORT);
        toast.setGravity(Gravity.CENTER, 0, 0);
        toast.show();
    } else {
        Log.d(TAG, "showKeypad: used=" + toPuzzleString(tiles));
        Dialog v = new Keypad(this, tiles, puzzleView);
        v.show();
    }
}
```

To decide which numbers are possible, we pass the Keypad a string in the extraData area containing all the numbers that have already been used.

Implementing the Game Logic

The rest of the code in Game.java concerns itself with the logic of the game, in particular with determining which are and aren't valid moves according to the rules. The setTileIfValid() method is a key part of that. Given an x and y position and the new value of a tile, it changes the tile only if the value provided is valid.

```
Sudokuv2/src/org/example/sudoku/Game.java
/** Change the tile only if it's a valid move */
protected boolean setTileIfValid(int x, int y, int value) {
    int tiles[] = getUsedTiles(x, y);
    if (value != 0) {
        for (int tile : tiles) {
            if (tile == value)
                return false;
        }
    }
    setTile(x, y, value);
    calculateUsedTiles();
    return true;
}
```

To detect valid moves, we create an array for every tile in the grid. For each position, it keeps a list of filled-in tiles that are currently visible from that position. If a number appears on the list, then it won't be valid for the current tile.

The getUsedTiles() method retrieves that list for a given tile position:

Sudokuv2/src/org/example/sudoku/Game.java

```
/** Cache of used tiles */
private final int used[][][] = new int[9][9][];

/** Return cached used tiles visible from the given coords */
protected int[] getUsedTiles(int x, int y) {
    return used[x][y];
}
```

The array of used tiles is somewhat expensive to compute, so we cache the array and recalculate it only when necessary by calling calculateUsedTiles():

Sudokuv2/src/org/example/sudoku/Game.java

```
/** Compute the two dimensional array of used tiles */
private void calculateUsedTiles() {
    for (int x = 0; x < 9; x++) {
        for (int y = 0; y < 9; y++) {
            used[x][y] = calculateUsedTiles(x, y);
            // Log.d(TAG, "used[" + x + "][" + y + "] = "
            // + toPuzzleString(used[x][y]));
        }
    }
}
```

calculateUsedTiles() simply calls calculateUsedTiles(x, y) on every position in the nine-by-nine grid:

Sudokuv2/src/org/example/sudoku/Game.java

```
Line 1   /** Compute the used tiles visible from this position */
         private int[] calculateUsedTiles(int x, int y) {
             int c[] = new int[9];
             // horizontal
      5      for (int i = 0; i < 9; i++) {
                 if (i == y)
                     continue;
                 int t = getTile(x, i);
                 if (t != 0)
     10              c[t - 1] = t;
             }
             // vertical
             for (int i = 0; i < 9; i++) {
                 if (i == x)
     15              continue;
                 int t = getTile(i, y);
```

```
         if (t != 0)
             c[t - 1] = t;
     }
20   // same cell block
     int startx = (x / 3) * 3;
     int starty = (y / 3) * 3;
     for (int i = startx; i < startx + 3; i++) {
         for (int j = starty; j < starty + 3; j++) {
25           if (i == x && j == y)
                 continue;
             int t = getTile(i, j);
             if (t != 0)
                 c[t - 1] = t;
30       }
     }
     // compress
     int nused = 0;
     for (int t : c) {
35       if (t != 0)
             nused++;
     }
     int c1[] = new int[nused];
     nused = 0;
40   for (int t : c) {
         if (t != 0)
             c1[nused++] = t;
     }
     return c1;
45  }
```

We start with an array of nine zeros. On line 5, we check all the tiles on the same horizontal row as the current tile, and if a tile is occupied, we stuff its number into the array:

On line 13, we do the same thing for all the tiles on the same vertical column, and on line 21, we do the same for tiles in the three-by-three block.

The last step, starting at line 33, is to compress the zeros out of the array before we return it. We do this so that array.length can be used to quickly tell how many used tiles are visible from the current position.

Miscellaneous

Here are a few other utility functions and variables that round out the implementation. easyPuzzle, mediumPuzzle, and hardPuzzle are our hard-coded Sudoku puzzles for easy, medium, and hard difficulty levels, respectively.

```
Sudokuv2/src/org/example/sudoku/Game.java
```

```java
private final String easyPuzzle =
    "360000000004230800000004200" +
    "070460003820000014500013020" +
    "001900000007048300000000045";
private final String mediumPuzzle =
    "650000070000506000014000005" +
    "007009000002314700000700800" +
    "500000630000201000030000097";
private final String hardPuzzle =
    "009000000080605020501078000" +
    "000000700706040102004000000" +
    "000720903090301080000000600";
```

getPuzzle() simply takes a difficulty level and returns a puzzle:

```
Sudokuv2/src/org/example/sudoku/Game.java
```

```java
/** Given a difficulty level, come up with a new puzzle */
private int[] getPuzzle(int diff) {
    String puz;
    // TODO: Continue last game
    switch (diff) {
    case DIFFICULTY_HARD:
        puz = hardPuzzle;
        break;
    case DIFFICULTY_MEDIUM:
        puz = mediumPuzzle;
        break;
    case DIFFICULTY_EASY:
    default:
        puz = easyPuzzle;
        break;
    }
    return fromPuzzleString(puz);
}
```

Later we'll change getPuzzle() to implement a continue function.

toPuzzleString() converts a puzzle from an array of integers to a string.
fromPuzzleString() does the opposite.

```
Sudokuv2/src/org/example/sudoku/Game.java
```

```java
/** Convert an array into a puzzle string */
static private String toPuzzleString(int[] puz) {
    StringBuilder buf = new StringBuilder();
    for (int element : puz) {
        buf.append(element);
    }
    return buf.toString();
}
```

```
/** Convert a puzzle string into an array */
static protected int[] fromPuzzleString(String string) {
    int[] puz = new int[string.length()];
    for (int i = 0; i < puz.length; i++) {
        puz[i] = string.charAt(i) - '0';
    }
    return puz;
}
```

The getTile() method takes x and y positions and returns the number currently occupying that tile. If it's zero, that means the tile is blank.

Sudokuv2/src/org/example/sudoku/Game.java

```
/** Return the tile at the given coordinates */
private int getTile(int x, int y) {
    return puzzle[y * 9 + x];
}


/** Change the tile at the given coordinates */
private void setTile(int x, int y, int value) {
    puzzle[y * 9 + x] = value;
}
```

getTileString() is used when displaying a tile. It will return either a string with the value of the tile or an empty string if the tile is blank.

Sudokuv2/src/org/example/sudoku/Game.java

```
/** Return a string for the tile at the given coordinates */
protected String getTileString(int x, int y) {
    int v = getTile(x, y);
    if (v == 0)
        return "";
    else
        return String.valueOf(v);
}
```

Once all these pieces are in place, you should have a playable Sudoku game. Give it a try to verify it works. As with any code, though, there is room for improvement.

4.5 Making More Improvements

Although the code presented in this chapter performs acceptably for a Sudoku game, more complex programs will likely need to be more carefully written in order to squeeze the last drop of performance out of the device. In particular, the onDraw() method is a very performance-critical piece of code, so it's best to do as little as possible there.

Here are some ideas for speeding up this method:

- If possible, avoid doing any object allocations in the method onDraw().
- Prefetch things such as color constants elsewhere (for example, in the view's constructor).
- Create your Paint objects up front, and just use existing instances in onDraw().
- For values used multiple times, such as the width returned by getWidth(), retrieve the value at the beginning of the method and then access it from your local copy.

As a further exercise for the reader, I encourage you to think about how you could make the Sudoku game graphically richer. For example, you could add some fireworks when the player solves the puzzle or make the tiles spin around like Vanna White does. A moving background behind the puzzle might be interesting. Let your imagination go wild. If you want to make a top-notch product, touches like this can add pizzazz to an otherwise ordinary offering.

In Chapter 5, *Multimedia*, on page 89, we'll enhance the program with a little mood music, and in Chapter 6, *Storing Local Data*, on page 105, we'll see how to remember the puzzle state and finally implement that Continue button.

4.6 Fast-Forward >>

In this chapter, we just scratched the surface of Android's graphics capabilities. The native 2D library is quite large, so as you're actually writing your programs, be sure to take advantage of the tooltips, auto-completion, and Javadoc provided by the Android Eclipse plug-in. The online documentation for the android.graphics[3] package goes into much more detail if you need it.

If your program needs more advanced graphics, you may want to look ahead a bit and read Chapter 10, *3D Graphics in OpenGL*, on page 181. There you'll find information on how to use Android's 3D graphics library, which is based on the OpenGL ES standard. Otherwise, turn to the next chapter for an introduction to the wonderful world of Android audio and video.

---

3. http://code.google.com/android/reference/android/graphics/package-summary.html

Chapter 5

Multimedia

Remember those Apple television ads with the silhouette people dancing wildly to the beat of their iPods? That's the kind of excitement you want your products to generate.[1] Music, sound effects, and video can make your programs more immersive and engaging than text and graphics alone.

This chapter will show you how to add multimedia to your Android application. You may not have your users cavorting in the aisles, but if you do it properly, you can at least put smiles on their faces.

5.1 Playing Audio

It was a dark and stormy night.... There goes the starting shot, and they're off.... The crowd goes wild as State sinks a three-pointer with one second remaining....

Audio cues permeate the environment and set the tempo for our emotions. Think of sound as another way to get into your user's head. Just like you use graphics on the display to convey some information to the user, you can use audio to back that up and reinforce it.

Android supports sound and music output through the MediaPlayer class in the android.media package.[2] Let's try it with a simple example that plays sounds when you press a key on the keyboard or D-pad.

---

1. Of course, normal people older than the age of 8 can't dance like that. Except perhaps that time when my kids put a lizard in my...but I digress.
2. http://code.google.com/android/toolbox/apis/media.html

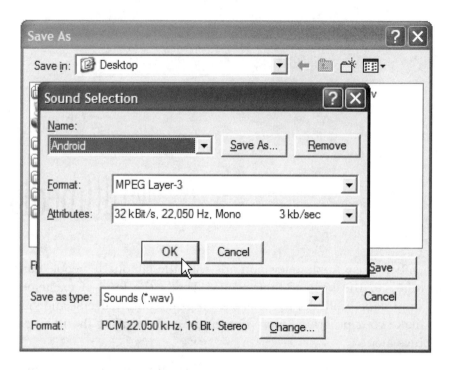

Figure 5.1: SAVE SOUND EFFECTS IN A COMPRESSED FORMAT THAT ANDROID CAN PLAY.

We'll start by creating a "Hello, Android" project, using the following parameters in the New Android Project dialog box:

```
Project name: Audio
Package name: org.example.audio
Activity name: Audio
Application name: Audio
```

Next we'll need a few sounds to play. For this example, I created my own with the Windows Sound Recorder program (Start > Programs > Accessories > Entertainment > Sound Recorder on Windows XP) and an inexpensive headset. After getting the sound levels right, I recorded each sound, selected File > Save As... from the menu, clicked the Change... button, and selected a format Android can recognize (see Figure 5.1). You can find all the sound files and source code for these examples on the book's website.

Copy the sound files into the res/raw directory of your project. As you recall from Section 2.4, *Using Resources*, on page 21, simply copying a

Figure 5.2: COPY AUDIO FILES INTO THE RES/RAW DIRECTORY OF YOUR PROJECT.

file into the res directory causes the Android Eclipse plug-in to define a Java symbol for you in the R class. When you're done, the project should look like Figure 5.2.

Now it's time to fill out the Audio activity. First we declare a new MediaPlayer instance for each sound and initialize the instances in the onCreate() method.

Joe Asks...

What Audio Formats Does Android Support?

Well, there's support on paper, there's support in the emulator, and there's support on the actual devices. On paper, Android supports the following file types (this is subject to change with new releases):

- WAV (PCM uncompressed)
- AAC (Apple iPod format, unprotected)
- MP3 (MPEG-3)
- WMA (Windows media audio)
- AMR (Speech codec)
- OGG (Ogg Vorbis)*
- MIDI (Instruments)

In reality, I've found that only the OGG, WAV, and MP3 formats work well in the emulator, and thus those are the only ones that I can recommend for application development. Android's native audio format appears to be 44.1kHz 16-bit stereo. However, since WAV files at that rate are huge, you should just stick to OGG or MP3 files (mono for voice or stereo for music). OGG files seem to work best for short clips like game sound effects.

Stay away from unusual rates like 8kHz because the resampling artifacts make those rates sound terrible. Use 11kHz, 22kHz, or 44.1kHz sampling rates for the best results. Remember that although the phone may have a tiny speaker, many of your users are going to be plugging in headphones (like an iPod), so you want your audio to be high quality.

---

*. http://www.vorbis.com

```
Audio/src/org/example/audio/Audio.java
package org.example.audio;

import android.app.Activity;
import android.media.MediaPlayer;
import android.os.Bundle;
import android.view.KeyEvent;

public class Audio extends Activity {
    private MediaPlayer up, down, left, right, enter;
    private MediaPlayer a, s, d, f;

    @Override
    public void onCreate(Bundle savedInstanceState) {
        super.onCreate(savedInstanceState);
        setContentView(R.layout.main);

        // Native rate is 44.1kHz 16 bit stereo, but
        // to save space we just use MPEG-3 22kHz mono
        up = MediaPlayer.create(this, R.raw.up);
        down = MediaPlayer.create(this, R.raw.down);
        left = MediaPlayer.create(this, R.raw.left);
        right = MediaPlayer.create(this, R.raw.right);
        enter = MediaPlayer.create(this, R.raw.enter);
        a = MediaPlayer.create(this, R.raw.a);
        s = MediaPlayer.create(this, R.raw.s);
        d = MediaPlayer.create(this, R.raw.d);
        f = MediaPlayer.create(this, R.raw.f);
    }
}
```

There are other ways to do this; for example, you could declare one MediaPlayer and keep reusing it. This would prevent sounds from overlapping, though, which may or may not be the effect you want.

Another method you may be tempted to try is to create a new MediaPlayer whenever you want to make a sound. However, this doesn't work in practice. For one thing, it slows the program down a little. Worse, in my testing it has a tendency to crash after playing just a few sounds. Therefore, I recommend you stick with the tried-and-true method of setting up your players ahead of time and playing them when needed.

Now that we have our sounds loaded up and ready to go, we just need to intercept the key presses and play the right sounds. We do that by overriding the Activity.onKeyDown() method.

Audio/src/org/example/audio/Audio.java

```
Line 1  @Override
        public boolean onKeyDown(int keyCode, KeyEvent event) {
            MediaPlayer mp;
            switch (keyCode) {
     5      case KeyEvent.KEYCODE_DPAD_UP:
                mp = up;
                break;
            case KeyEvent.KEYCODE_DPAD_DOWN:
                mp = down;
    10          break;
            case KeyEvent.KEYCODE_DPAD_LEFT:
                mp = left;
                break;
            case KeyEvent.KEYCODE_DPAD_RIGHT:
    15          mp = right;
                break;
            case KeyEvent.KEYCODE_DPAD_CENTER:
            case KeyEvent.KEYCODE_ENTER:
                mp = enter;
    20          break;
            case KeyEvent.KEYCODE_A:
                mp = a;
                break;
            case KeyEvent.KEYCODE_S:
    25          mp = s;
                break;
            case KeyEvent.KEYCODE_D:
                mp = d;
                break;
    30      case KeyEvent.KEYCODE_F:
                mp = f;
                break;
            default:
                return super.onKeyDown(keyCode, event);
    35      }
            mp.seekTo(0);
            mp.start();
            return true;
        }
```

The first part of the method selects a media player based on which key you pressed. Then on line 36, we call the seekTo() method to rewind the sound and the start() method to begin playing it. The start() method is asynchronous, so it returns immediately regardless of how long the sound lasts. If you like, you can use setOnCompletionListener() to be notified when the clip is finished.

When Things Go Wrong

If you do much multimedia programming, you'll soon discover that Android's MediaPlayer is a fickle beast. It will crash at the slightest provocation, such as calling its methods out of order or passing it an unrecognized format. One reason this happens is that MediaPlayer is mostly a native application with a thin layer of Java on top of it. The native player code is optimized for performance, and it doesn't seem to do much error checking.

Fortunately, Android's strong Linux process protections prevent any harm from being done if a crash occurs. The emulator (or the phone if you're running on a real device) and other applications will continue to run normally. The user would just see the application go away, possibly with a dialog box containing an error message.

During development, though, you can get considerably more diagnostic information to help you determine what went wrong. Messages and tracebacks will be printed to the Android system log, which you can view with the LogCat view in Eclipse or the adb logcat command (see Section 3.10, *Debugging with Log Messages*, on page 53).

If you run the program now and then press one of the keys (for example, the Enter key or the center D-pad key), you should hear a sound. If you don't hear anything, check your volume control (don't laugh), or look at the debugging messages in the LogCat view.[3]

For our next trick, we'll play a movie using only one line of code.

5.2 Playing Video

Video is more than just a bunch of pictures shown one right after another. It's sound as well, and the sound has to be closely synchronized with the images.

---

3. Audio output may be choppy or delayed in some cases. Try different formats (such as OGG instead of MP3) and lower bit rates. You may also want to investigate using the SoundPool class, which explicitly supports simultaneous streams. Unfortunately, it is buggy and poorly documented in the 1.0 release.

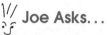

Joe Asks...

What Kind of Video Can You Watch on Android?

As with audio, format support is spotty with current versions of the Android SDK. Here's what is officially supported:

- MP4 (MPEG-4 low bit rate)
- H.263
- H.264 (AVC)

On a Windows machine, the only format that works reliably for me is MP4, so I recommend sticking with that for now. You can use a program like QuickTime Pro* to convert video from one format to another. Use the lowest resolution and bit rate that you can in order to save space, but don't set it so low that you sacrifice quality.

---

*. http://www.apple.com/quicktime/pro

Android's MediaPlayer class works with video the same way it does with plain audio. The only difference is that you need to create a Surface for the player to use to draw the images. You can use the start() and stop() methods to control playback.

I'm not going to show you another MediaPlayer example, however, because there is a simpler way to embed videos in your application: the VideoView class. To demonstrate it, create a new Android project called Video using these parameters:

```
Project name: Video
Package name: org.example.video
Activity name: Video
Application name: Video
```

Change the layout (res/layout/main.xml) to this:

Videov1/res/layout/main.xml

```
<?xml version="1.0" encoding="utf-8"?>
<FrameLayout
    xmlns:android="http://schemas.android.com/apk/res/android"
    android:layout_width="fill_parent"
    android:layout_height="fill_parent">
    <VideoView
        android:id="@+id/video"
```

Figure 5.3: EMBEDDING A VIDEO IS EASY WITH VIDEOVIEW.

```
        android:layout_height="wrap_content"
        android:layout_width="wrap_content"
        android:layout_gravity="center" />
</FrameLayout>
```

Open Video.java, and change the onCreate() method as follows:

Videov1/src/org/example/video/Video.java

```
package org.example.video;

import android.app.Activity;
import android.os.Bundle;
import android.widget.VideoView;

public class Video extends Activity {
    @Override
    public void onCreate(Bundle savedInstanceState) {
        super.onCreate(savedInstanceState);

        // Fill view from resource
        setContentView(R.layout.main);
        VideoView video = (VideoView) findViewById(R.id.video);

        // Load and start the movie
        video.setVideoPath("/data/samplevideo.mp4");
    }
}
```

The setVideoPath() method opens the file, sizes it to its container while preserving the aspect ratio, and begins playing it.

Now you need to upload something to play. To do that, run the following command:

```
C:\> adb push c:\code\samplevideo.mp4 /data/samplevideo.mp4
377 KB/s (0 bytes in 824192.002s)
```

You can find samplevideo.mp4 in the download package for this book, or you can create one of your own. The directory used here (/data) is just for illustrative purposes and should not really be used for media files.

Note that Android doesn't seem to care what extension you give the file. You can also upload and download files in Eclipse with the File Explorer view in the Android perspective, but I find the command line to be easier for simple things like this.

There's one more thing: we'd like the video to take over the whole screen including the title bar and status bar. To do that, all you need to do is specify the right theme in AndroidManifest.xml:

Video1/AndroidManifest.xml

```xml
<?xml version="1.0" encoding="utf-8"?>
<manifest xmlns:android="http://schemas.android.com/apk/res/android"
    package="org.example.video"
    android:versionCode="1"
    android:versionName="1.0.0">
  <application android:icon="@drawable/icon"
      android:label="@string/app_name">
    <activity android:name=".Video"
        android:label="@string/app_name"
        android:theme="@android:style/Theme.NoTitleBar.Fullscreen">
      <intent-filter>
        <action android:name="android.intent.action.MAIN" />
        <category android:name="android.intent.category.LAUNCHER" />
      </intent-filter>
    </activity>
  </application>
</manifest>
```

Once all that is done, when you run the program, you should see and hear the movie clip (see Figure 5.3, on the preceding page). Try rotating the display to verify it works in both portrait and landscape modes. *Voila!* Instant video goodness.

Now let's polish up the Sudoku sample with a little mood music.

Joe Asks...

Why Does It Restart the Video When I Rotate the Display?

Android assumes by default that your program knows nothing about screen rotations. To pick up possible resource changes, Android destroys and re-creates your activity from scratch. That means onCreate() is called again, which means the video is started again (as this example is currently written).

This behavior will be fine for 90 percent of all applications, so most developers will not have to worry about it. It's even a useful way to test your application life-cycle and state-saving/restoring code (see Section 2.2, *It's Alive!*, on page 16). However, there are a couple of ways to be smarter and optimize the transition.

The simplest way is to implement onRetainNonConfigurationInstance() in your activity to save some data that will be kept across the calls to onDestroy() and onCreate(). When you come back, you use getLastNonConfigurationInstance() in the new instance of your activity to recover that information. You can keep anything, even references to your current intent and running threads.

The more complicated way is to use the android:configChanges= property in AndroidManifest.xml to inform Android which changes you can handle. For example, if you set it to *keyboardHidden|orientation*, then Android will not destroy and re-create your activity when the user flips the keyboard. Instead, it will call onConfigurationChanged(Configuration) and assume you know what you're doing.*

---

*. For more details, see http://code.google.com/android/reference/android/app/Activity.html#ConfigurationChanges.

Sudoku Trivia

Dozens of Sudoku variants exist, although none has gained the popularity of the original. One uses a sixteen-by-sixteen grid, with hexadecimal numbers. Another, called Gattai 5 or Samurai Sudoku, uses five nine-by-nine grids that overlap at the corner regions.

5.3 Adding Sounds to Sudoku

In this section, we're going to take what we've learned and add background music to the Sudoku game we've been building. One song will play during the opening screen, and another will play during the actual game. This will demonstrate not just how to play music but also some important life-cycle considerations.

To add music to the main screen, we just need to override these two methods in the Sudoku class:

`Sudokuv3/src/org/example/sudoku/Sudoku.java`

```
@Override
protected void onResume() {
    super.onResume();
    Music.play(this, R.raw.main);
}

@Override
protected void onPause() {
    super.onPause();
    Music.stop(this);
}
```

If you recall from Section 2.2, *It's Alive!*, on page 16, the onResume() method is called when the activity is ready to begin interacting with the user. This is a good place to start up the music, so we put a Music.start() call there. The Music class will be defined shortly.

R.raw.main refers to res/raw/main.mp3. You can find these sound files in the Sudokuv3 project of the downloadable samples on the book's website.

The onPause() method is the paired bookend for onResume(). Android pauses the current activity prior to resuming a new one, so in Sudoku,

ᐯᐟᐟ Joe Asks...

Shouldn't We Use a Background Service for Music?

We haven't said much about the Android Service class, but you may have seen it used in some music-playing examples on the Web. Basically, a Service is a way to start a background process (a Linux daemon) that will run even after your current activity finishes. If you're writing a general-purpose music player and want the music to continue while you're reading mail or browsing the Web, then, yes, a Service would be appropriate. In most cases, though, you want the music to end when your program ends, so you don't need to use the Service class.

when you start a new game, the Sudoku activity will be paused, and then the Game activity will be started. onPause() will also be called when the user presses the Back or Home key. These are all places where we want our title music to stop, so we call Music.stop() in onPause().

Now let's do something similar for the music on the Game activity:

Sudokuv3/src/org/example/sudoku/Game.java

```java
@Override
protected void onResume() {
    super.onResume();
    Music.play(this, R.raw.game);
}

@Override
protected void onPause() {
    super.onPause();
    Music.stop(this);
}
```

If you compare this to what we did to the Sudoku class, you'll notice that we're referencing a different sound resource, R.raw.game (res/raw/game.mp3).

The final piece of the musical puzzle is the Music class, which will manage the MediaPlayer class used to play the current music:

```
Sudokuv3/src/org/example/sudoku/Music.java
```

```
Line 1   package org.example.sudoku;

         import android.content.Context;
         import android.media.MediaPlayer;

   5
         public class Music {
             private static MediaPlayer mp = null;

             /** Stop old song and start new one */
  10         public static void play(Context context, int resource) {
                 stop(context);
                 mp = MediaPlayer.create(context, resource);
                 mp.setLooping(true);
                 mp.start();
  15         }

             /** Stop the music */
             public static void stop(Context context) {
                 if (mp != null) {
  20                 mp.stop();
                     mp.release();
                     mp = null;
                 }
             }
  25     }
```

The play() method first calls the stop() method to halt whatever music is currently playing. Next, it creates a new MediaPlayer instance using MediaPlayer.create(), passing it a context and a resource ID.

After we have a player, we then set an option to make it repeat the music in a loop and then start it playing. The start() method comes back immediately.

The stop() method that begins on line 18 is simple. After a little defensive check to make sure we actually have a MediaPlayer to work with, we call its stop() and release() methods. The MediaPlayer.stop() method, strangely enough, stops the music. The release() method frees system resources associated with the player. Since those are native resources, we can't wait until normal Java garbage collection reclaims them. Leaving out release() is a good way to make your program fail unexpectedly (not that this has ever happened to me, of course; I'm just saying *you* should keep that in mind).

Now comes the fun part—try playing Sudoku with these changes in place. Stress test it in every way you can imagine, such as switching to different activities, pressing the Back button and the Home button from different points in the game, starting the program when it's already running at different points, and so forth. Proper life cycle management is a pain sometimes, but your users will appreciate the effort.

5.4 Fast-Forward >>

In this chapter, we covered playing audio and video clips using the Android SDK. We didn't discuss recording because most programs will not need to do that, but if you happen to be the exception, then look up the MediaRecorder class in the online documentation.[4]

In Chapter 6, *Storing Local Data*, on page 105, you'll learn about some simple ways Android programs can store data between invocations. If you don't need to do that, then you can skip ahead to Chapter 7, *The Connected World*, on page 117 and learn about network access.

---

4. http://code.google.com/android/reference/android/media/MediaRecorder.html

Storing Local Data

So far, we've concentrated on writing applications that don't need to keep data around when they exit. They start up, run, and go away, leaving no trace that they were ever there. However, most real programs need persistent state, whether it's a simple font size setting, an embarrassing photo from your last office party, or next week's meal plan. Whatever it is, Android lets you permanently store it on your mobile device for later use and protects it from accidental or malicious access by other programs.

Your application can store data using several different techniques depending on the size of the data, its structure, its lifetime, and whether it will be shared with other programs. In this chapter, we'll take a look at three simple methods to keep local data: the preferences API, instance state bundles, and flash memory files. In Chapter 9, *Putting SQL to Work*, on page 161, we'll delve into more advanced techniques using the built-in SQLite database engine.

6.1 Adding Options to Sudoku

In Section 3.7, *Adding a Menu*, on page 46, we used the onCreateOptionsMenu() method to add a menu containing one item to the main Sudoku screen. When the user presses the Menu key and selects the Settings... item, the code starts the Settings activity, which lets the user change the options for the game. Because Settings extends PreferenceActivity, the values for the settings are stored in the program's preferences area, but originally we didn't do anything with them. Now we're going to implement them.

> ### Sudoku Trivia
>
> There are 6,670,903,752,021,072,936,960 possible classic Sudoku solution grids. If you eliminate duplicates that are just rotations, reflections, or relabelings of each other, you're left with "only" 5,472,730,538 solutions.

First let's modify the Settings class to add a couple of getter methods that retrieve the current values of our two options. Here's the new definition:

Sudokuv4/src/org/example/sudoku/Settings.java

```java
package org.example.sudoku;

import android.content.Context;
import android.os.Bundle;
import android.preference.PreferenceActivity;
import android.preference.PreferenceManager;

public class Settings extends PreferenceActivity {
    // Option names and default values
    private static final String OPT_MUSIC = "music";
    private static final boolean OPT_MUSIC_DEF = true;
    private static final String OPT_HINTS = "hints";
    private static final boolean OPT_HINTS_DEF = true;

    @Override
    protected void onCreate(Bundle savedInstanceState) {
        super.onCreate(savedInstanceState);
        addPreferencesFromResource(R.xml.settings);
    }

    /** Get the current value of the music option */
    public static boolean getMusic(Context context) {
        return PreferenceManager.getDefaultSharedPreferences(context)
                .getBoolean(OPT_MUSIC, OPT_MUSIC_DEF);
    }

    /** Get the current value of the hints option */
    public static boolean getHints(Context context) {
        return PreferenceManager.getDefaultSharedPreferences(context)
                .getBoolean(OPT_HINTS, OPT_HINTS_DEF);
    }
}
```

Be careful that the option keys (music and hints) match the keys used in res/xml/settings.xml.

Music.play() has to be modified to check for the music preference:

Sudokuv4/src/org/example/sudoku/Music.java

```
/** Stop old song and start new one */
public static void play(Context context, int resource) {
   stop(context);

   // Start music only if not disabled in preferences
   if (Settings.getMusic(context)) {
      mp = MediaPlayer.create(context, resource);
      mp.setLooping(true);
      mp.start();
   }
}
```

And PuzzleView.onDraw() also needs to be modified to check for the hints preference:

Sudokuv4/src/org/example/sudoku/PuzzleView.java

```
if (Settings.getHints(getContext())) {
   // Draw the hints...
}
```

If getHints() returns true, we draw the highlights for the hints, as shown in Figure 4.6, on page 76. Otherwise, we just skip that part.

Next I'll show you how to use the preferences API to store things other than just options.

6.2 Continuing an Old Game

At any time the player can decide to quit playing our Sudoku game and go do something else. Maybe their boss walked in, or they got a phone call or a notification of an important appointment. Whatever the reason, we want to allow the player to come back later and continue where they left off.

First we need to save the current state of the puzzle somewhere. The preferences API can be used for more than just options; it can store any small stand-alone bits of information that go with your program. In this case, the state of the puzzle can be saved as a string of eighty-one characters, one for each tile.

In the Game class, we'll start by defining a couple of constants—one for the puzzle data key and one for a flag to tell us to continue the previous game rather than start a new one.

```
Sudokuv4/src/org/example/sudoku/Game.java
```

```java
private static final String PREF_PUZZLE = "puzzle" ;
protected static final int DIFFICULTY_CONTINUE = -1;
```

Next we need to save the current puzzle whenever the game is paused. See Section 2.2, *It's Alive!*, on page 16 for a description of onPause() and the other life-cycle methods.

```
Sudokuv4/src/org/example/sudoku/Game.java
```

```java
@Override
protected void onPause() {
    super.onPause();
    Log.d(TAG, "onPause");
    Music.stop(this);

    // Save the current puzzle
    getPreferences(MODE_PRIVATE).edit().putString(PREF_PUZZLE,
            toPuzzleString(puzzle)).commit();
}
```

Now the puzzle is saved, but how do we read the saved data? Remember that when the game is started, the getPuzzle() method is called, and the difficulty level is passed in. We'll use that for continuing as well.

```
Sudokuv4/src/org/example/sudoku/Game.java
```

```java
/** Given a difficulty level, come up with a new puzzle */
private int[] getPuzzle(int diff) {
    String puz;
    switch (diff) {
    case DIFFICULTY_CONTINUE:
        puz = getPreferences(MODE_PRIVATE).getString(PREF_PUZZLE,
                easyPuzzle);
        break;
        // ...
    }
    return fromPuzzleString(puz);
}
```

All we need to do is add a check for DIFFICULTY_CONTINUE. If that is set, then instead of starting with a fresh puzzle, we read the one we stuffed into the preferences.

Next, we need to make the Continue button on the main screen (see Figure 3.4, on page 37) actually do something. Here is where we set that up.

```
Sudokuv4/src/org/example/sudoku/Sudoku.java
```

```java
public void onClick(View v) {
    switch (v.getId()) {
    case R.id.continue_button:
        startGame(Game.DIFFICULTY_CONTINUE);
        break;
        // ...
    }
}
```

We added a case in Sudoku.onClick() to call startGame() when the Continue button is pressed, passing it DIFFICULTY_CONTINUE. startGame() passes the difficulty to the Game activity, and Game.onCreate() calls Intent.getIntExtra() to read the difficulty and passes that to getPuzzle() (you can see the code for that in Section 4.2, *Starting the Game*, on page 62).

There's one more thing to do: restore from our saved game when our activity goes away and comes back on its own (such as if another activity is started and then the user comes back to the Game activity). This modification to the Game.onCreate() method will take care of that:

```
Sudokuv4/src/org/example/sudoku/Game.java
```

```java
@Override
protected void onCreate(Bundle savedInstanceState) {
    // ...
    // If the activity is restarted, do a continue next time
    getIntent().putExtra(KEY_DIFFICULTY, DIFFICULTY_CONTINUE);
}
```

That pretty much covers it for preferences. Next let's look at saving instance state.

6.3 Remembering the Current Position

If you change the screen orientation while Sudoku is running, you'll notice that it forgets where its cursor is. That's because we use a custom PuzzleView view. Normal Android views save their view state automatically, but since we made our own, we don't get that for free.

Unlike persistent state, instance state is not permanent. It lives in a Bundle class on Android's application stack. Instance state is intended to be used for small bits of information such as cursor positions.

Here's what we have to do to implement it:

Sudokuv4/src/org/example/sudoku/PuzzleView.java

```
Line 1    private static final String SELX = "selX";
     -    private static final String SELY = "selY";
     -    private static final String VIEW_STATE = "viewState";
     -    private static final int ID = 42;

     5
     -    public PuzzleView(Context context) {
     -        // ...
     -        setId(ID);
     -    }

    10
     -    @Override
     -    protected Parcelable onSaveInstanceState() {
     -        Parcelable p = super.onSaveInstanceState();
     -        Log.d(TAG, "onSaveInstanceState");
    15        Bundle bundle = new Bundle();
     -        bundle.putInt(SELX, selX);
     -        bundle.putInt(SELY, selY);
     -        bundle.putParcelable(VIEW_STATE, p);
     -        return bundle;
    20    }
     -    @Override
     -    protected void onRestoreInstanceState(Parcelable state) {
     -        Log.d(TAG, "onRestoreInstanceState");
     -        Bundle bundle = (Bundle) state;
    25        select(bundle.getInt(SELX), bundle.getInt(SELY));
     -        super.onRestoreInstanceState(bundle.getParcelable(VIEW_STATE));
     -        return;
     -    }
```

On line 1, we define some constants for keys to save and restore the cursor position. We need to save both our own x and y positions, plus any state needed by the underlying View class.

As part of Activity.onSaveInstanceState() processing, Android will walk down the view hierarchy and call View.onSaveInstanceState() on every view it finds that has an ID. The same thing happens for onRestoreInstanceState(). Normally, this ID would come from XML, but since PuzzleView was created in code, we need to set it ourselves. We make up an arbitrary number on line 4 (any value will do as long as it's positive) and then use the setId() method to assign it on line 8.

The onSaveInstanceState() method is defined on line 12. We call the superclass to get its state, and then we save ours and theirs in a Bundle. Failing to call the superclass will result in a runtime error.

Later, onRestoreInstanceState() (line 22) will be called to tease out the information we saved. We get our own x and y positions from the Bundle, and then we call the superclass to let it get whatever it needs. After making these changes, the cursor will be remembered by PuzzleView, just like any other Android view.

Next let's look at keeping data in plain old files.

6.4 Accessing the Internal File System

Android runs Linux under the covers, so there's a real file system mounted in there with a root directory and everything. The files are stored on nonvolatile flash memory built into the device, so they are not lost when the phone is turned off.

All of the usual Java file I/O routines from the java.io package are available for your program to use, with the caveat that your process has limited permissions so it can't mess up any other application's data. In fact, the main thing it can access is a package private directory created at install time (/data/data/*packagename*).

A few helper methods are provided on the Context class (and thus on the Activity class extended by each of your activities) to let you read and write data there. Here are the ones you're most likely to need:

deleteFile()	Delete a private file. Returns true if it worked, false otherwise.
fileList()	Return a list of all files in the application's private area in a String array.
openFileInput()	Open a private file for reading. Returns a java.io.FileInputStream.
openFileOutput()	Open a private file for writing. Returns a java.io.FileOutputStream.

However, since this internal memory is limited, I recommend you keep the size of any data you put there low, say a megabyte or two at the most, and carefully handle I/O errors when writing in case the space runs out.

Luckily, internal memory isn't the only storage that you have to work with.

All in the Family

If you recall from Section 2.5, *Safe and Secure*, on page 22, each application normally gets its own user ID at install time. That user ID is the only one that is allowed to read and write from the application's private directory. However, if two applications are signed* by the same digital certificate, then Android assumes they are from the same developer and gives them the same user ID.

On the one hand, that allows them to share all sorts of data with each other if they so choose. But on the other, it also means they'll need to take special care to stay out of each other's way.

*. http://code.google.com/android/devel/security.html#signing

6.5 Accessing SD Cards

Some Android devices will include a slot for additional flash memory to be plugged in, typically a Secure Digital (SD) card. These memory cards, if present, are much larger than the built-in memory, and thus they're ideal for storing multimegabyte music and video files. They cannot be used for code, and every application can read and write files there.

In Section 5.2, *Playing Video*, on page 95, we uploaded a sample video file to the /data directory of the emulated device. This is the wrong place for it, since we're not supposed to put large files on the internal file system. So, now I'm going to show you a better way.

The first step is to create and format a virtual SD card that we can "plug in" to the emulator. For this, we use the mksdcard utility:[1]

```
C:\> mksdcard 256M c:\temp\sd.img
C:\> dir c:\temp\sd.img
 Volume in drive C is ANDROID_RULES
 Volume Serial Number is 5432-ABCD

 Directory of c:\temp

11/17/2008  08:58 PM       268,435,456 sd.img
             1 File(s)      268,435,456 bytes
             0 Dir(s)     4,369,543,168 bytes free
```

---

1. http://code.google.com/android/reference/othertools.html#mksdcard

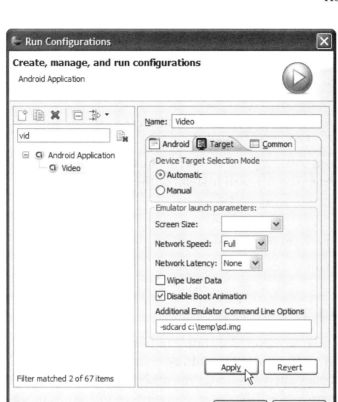

Figure 6.1: SPECIFY THE PATH NAME FOR THE SD CARD IMAGE IN THE EMULATOR OPTIONS.

This creates a virtual SD card on your development machine that can hold up to 256 megabytes. You can make it any size you like, but if you make it too small, it may cause the emulator to crash; if you make it too big, you'll just waste space on your computer's disk drive.

After creating the image file for the card, you need to tell the Android emulator where to find it. Unlike a real phone, you'll need to restart the emulated device in order to plug in the card. Close the emulator window if it's open, and then edit the Eclipse launch configuration for the Video project (Run > Run Configurations... in Eclipse 3.4). Add the option as shown in Figure 6.1, and then select Run:

```
-sdcard c:\temp\sd.img
```

If you're not using Eclipse, then just add the option to your emulator command line manually.

Once the emulator is running again, let's copy the sample video to the SD card:

```
C:\> adb push c:\code\samplevideo.mp4 /sdcard/samplevideo.mp4
140 KB/s (0 bytes in 824192.005s)
```

Then we need to modify the onCreate() method of the Video class to play the movie from the SD card instead of the /data directory:

Videov2/src/org/example/video/Video.java

```
// Load and start the movie
video.setVideoPath("/sdcard/samplevideo.mp4");
```

Now try to run the program. The video should play normally.

6.6 Fast-Forward >>

In this chapter, we covered a couple of basic ways to store local data on the Android platform. That should be enough to get you started, but for structured data such as phone lists and recipes, you'll need something more advanced. See Chapter 9, *Putting SQL to Work*, on page 161 for directions on how to use Android's built-in SQLite database and how to share information between applications using content providers.

This brings us to the end of Part II. With the help of the Sudoku example, you've learned all the basics of Android programming, including user interfaces, 2D graphics, audio, video, and simple data storage.

Now it's time to leave Sudoku behind and move beyond the basics.

Part III

Beyond the Basics

Chapter 7

The Connected World

Over the next few chapters, we'll cover more advanced topics such as network access and location-based services. You can write many useful applications without these features, but going beyond the basic features of Android will really help you add value to your programs, giving them much more functionality with a minimum of effort.

What do you use your mobile phone for? Aside from making calls, more and more people are using their phones as mobile Internet devices. Analysts predict that in a few years mobile phones will surpass desktop computers as the number-one way to connect to the Internet.[1] This point has already been reached in some parts of the world.[2]

Android phones are well equipped for the new connected world of the mobile Internet. First, Android provides a full-featured web browser based on the WebKit open source project.[3] This is the same engine you will find in Google Chrome, the Apple iPhone, and the Safari desktop browser but with a twist. Android lets you use the browser as a component right inside your application.

Second, Android gives your programs access to standard network services like TCP/IP sockets. This lets you consume web services from Google, Yahoo, Amazon, and many other sources on the Internet.

---

1. http://www.idc.com/getdoc.jsp?containerId=prUS21303808
2. http://www.comscore.com/press/release.asp?press=1742
3. http://webkit.org

Figure 7.1: OPENING A BROWSER USING AN ANDROID INTENT

In this chapter, you'll learn how to take advantage of all these features and more through four example programs:

- BrowserIntent: Demonstrates opening an external web browser using an Android intent
- BrowserView: Shows you how to embed a browser directly into your application
- LocalBrowser: Explains how JavaScript in an embedded WebView and Java code in your Android program can talk to each other
- Translate: Uses data binding, threading, and web services for an amusing purpose

7.1 Browsing by Intent

The simplest thing you can do with Android's networking API is to open a browser on a web page of your choice. You might want to do this to provide a link to your home page from your program or to access some server-based application such as an ordering system. In Android all it takes is three lines of code.

To demonstrate, let's write a new example called BrowserIntent, which will have an edit field where you can enter a URL and a Go button you press to open the browser on that URL (see Figure 7.1).

Start by creating a new "Hello, Android" project with the following values in the New Project wizard:

```
Project name: BrowserIntent
Package name: org.example.browserintent
Activity name: BrowserIntent
Application name: BrowserIntent
```

Once you have a the basic program, change the layout file (res/layout/main.xml) so it looks like this:

BrowserIntent/res/layout/main.xml

```xml
<?xml version="1.0" encoding="utf-8"?>
<LinearLayout
    xmlns:android="http://schemas.android.com/apk/res/android"
    android:orientation="horizontal"
    android:layout_width="fill_parent"
    android:layout_height="fill_parent">
    <EditText
        android:id="@+id/url_field"
        android:layout_width="wrap_content"
        android:layout_height="wrap_content"
        android:layout_weight="1.0"
        android:lines="1" />
    <Button
        android:id="@+id/go_button"
        android:layout_width="wrap_content"
        android:layout_height="wrap_content"
        android:text="@string/go_button" />
</LinearLayout>
```

This defines our two controls, an EditText control and a Button.

On EditText, we set android:layout_weight="1.0" to make the text area fill up all the horizontal space to the left of the button, and we also set android:lines="1" to limit the height of the control to one vertical line. Note that this has no effect on the amount of text the user can enter here, just the way it is displayed.

As always, human-readable text should be put in a resource file, res/values/strings.xml:

BrowserIntent/res/values/strings.xml

```xml
<?xml version="1.0" encoding="utf-8"?>
<resources>
    <string name="app_name">BrowserIntent</string>
    <string name="go_button">Go</string>
</resources>
```

Next we need to fill in the onCreate() method in the BrowserIntent class. This is where we'll build the user interface and hook up all the behavior. If you don't feel like typing all this in, the complete source code for the examples is available online.

BrowserIntent/src/org/example/browserintent/BrowserIntent.java

```
Line 1   package org.example.browserintent;

    -    import android.app.Activity;
    -    import android.content.Intent;
    5    import android.net.Uri;
    -    import android.os.Bundle;
    -    import android.view.KeyEvent;
    -    import android.view.View;
    -    import android.view.View.OnClickListener;
    10   import android.view.View.OnKeyListener;
    -    import android.widget.Button;
    -    import android.widget.EditText;

    -    public class BrowserIntent extends Activity {
    15       private EditText urlText;
    -        private Button goButton;

    -        @Override
    -        public void onCreate(Bundle savedInstanceState) {
    20           super.onCreate(savedInstanceState);
    -            setContentView(R.layout.main);

    -            // Get a handle to all user interface elements
    -            urlText = (EditText) findViewById(R.id.url_field);
    25           goButton = (Button) findViewById(R.id.go_button);

    -            // Setup event handlers
    -            goButton.setOnClickListener(new OnClickListener() {
    -                public void onClick(View view) {
    30                   openBrowser();
    -                }
    -            });
    -            urlText.setOnKeyListener(new OnKeyListener() {
    -                public boolean onKey(View view, int keyCode, KeyEvent event) {
    35                   if (keyCode == KeyEvent.KEYCODE_ENTER) {
    -                        openBrowser();
    -                        return true;
    -                    }
    -                    return false;
    40               }
    -            });
    -        }
    -    }
```

Inside onCreate(), we call setContentView() on line 21 to load the view from its definition in the layout resource, and then we call findViewById() on line 24 to get a handle to our two user interface controls.

Line 28 tells Android to run some code when the user selects the Go button, either by touching it or by navigating to it and pressing the center D-pad button. When that happens, we call the openBrowser() method, which will be defined in a moment.

As a convenience, if the user types an address and hits the Enter key (if their phone has one), we want the browser to open just like they had clicked Go. To do this, we define a listener starting on line 33 that will be called every time the user types a keystroke into the edit field. If it's the enter key, then we call the openBrowser() method to open the browser; otherwise, we return false to let the text control handle the key normally.

Now comes the part you've been waiting for: the openBrowser() method. As promised, it's three lines long:

BrowserIntent/src/org/example/browserintent/BrowserIntent.java

```
/** Open a browser on the URL specified in the text box */
private void openBrowser() {
    Uri uri = Uri.parse(urlText.getText().toString());
    Intent intent = new Intent(Intent.ACTION_VIEW, uri);
    startActivity(intent);
}
```

The first line retrieves the address of the web page as a string (for example, "http://www.android.com") and converts it to a uniform resource identifier (URI). The next line creates a new Intent class with an action of VIEW_ACTION, passing it the Uri class just created as the object we want to view. Finally, we call the startActivity() method to request that this action be performed.

When the Browser activity starts, it will create its own view (see Figure 7.2, on the following page), and your program will be paused. If the user presses the Back key at that point, the browser window will go away, and your application will continue. But what if you want to see some of your user interface and a web page at the same time? Android allows you to do that by using the WebView class.

7.2 Web with a View

On your desktop computer, a web browser is a large, complicated, memory-gobbling program with all sorts of features like bookmarks, plug-ins, Flash animations, tabs, scroll bars, printing, and so forth.

Figure 7.2: VIEWING A WEB PAGE WITH THE DEFAULT BROWSER

When I was working on the Eclipse project and someone suggested replacing some common text views with embedded web browsers, I thought they were crazy. Wouldn't it make more sense, I argued, to simply enhance the text viewer to do italics or tables or whatever it was that was missing?

It turns out they weren't crazy because:

- A web browser can be (relatively) lean and mean if you strip out everything but the basic rendering engine.
- If you enhance a text view to add more and more things that a browser engine can do, you end up with either an overly complicated, bloated text viewer or an underpowered browser.

Android provides a wrapper around the WebKit browser engine called WebView that you can use to get the real power of a browser with as little as 1MB of overhead. Although 1MB is still significant on an embedded device, there are many cases where using a WebView is appropriate.

WebView works pretty much like any other Android view except that it has a few extra methods specific to the browser. I'm going to show you how it works by doing an embedded version of the previous example. This one will be called BrowserView instead of BrowserIntent, since it uses an embedded View instead of an Intent.

Start by creating a new "Hello, Android" project using these settings:

```
Project name: BrowserView
Package name: org.example.browserview
Activity name: BrowserView
Application name: BrowserView
```

The layout file for BrowserView is similar to the one in BrowserIntent, except we've added a WebView at the bottom:

BrowserView/res/layout/main.xml

```xml
<?xml version="1.0" encoding="utf-8"?>
<LinearLayout
    xmlns:android="http://schemas.android.com/apk/res/android"
    android:orientation="vertical"
    android:layout_width="fill_parent"
    android:layout_height="fill_parent">
    <LinearLayout
        android:orientation="horizontal"
        android:layout_width="fill_parent"
        android:layout_height="wrap_content">
        <EditText
            android:id="@+id/url_field"
            android:layout_width="wrap_content"
            android:layout_height="wrap_content"
            android:layout_weight="1.0"
            android:lines="1" />
        <Button
            android:id="@+id/go_button"
            android:layout_width="wrap_content"
            android:layout_height="wrap_content"
            android:text="@string/go_button" />
    </LinearLayout>
    <WebView
        android:id="@+id/web_view"
        android:layout_width="fill_parent"
        android:layout_height="wrap_content"
        android:layout_weight="1.0" />
</LinearLayout>
```

We use two LinearLayout controls to make everything appear in the right place. The outermost control divides the screen into top and bottom regions; the top has the text area and button, and the bottom has the

WebView. The innermost LinearLayout is the same as before; it just makes the text area go on the left and the button on the right.

The onCreate() method for BrowserView is exactly the same as before, except that now there is one extra view to look up:

`BrowserView/src/org/example/browserview/BrowserView.java`

```
import android.webkit.WebView;
// ...

public class BrowserView extends Activity {
    private WebView webView;
    // ...
    @Override
    public void onCreate(Bundle savedInstanceState) {
        // ...
        webView = (WebView) findViewById(R.id.web_view);
        // ...
    }
}
```

The openBrowser() method, however, is different:

`BrowserView/src/org/example/browserview/BrowserView.java`

```
/** Open a browser on the URL specified in the text box */
private void openBrowser() {
    webView.loadUrl(urlText.getText().toString());
    webView.requestFocus();
}
```

The loadUrl() method causes the browser engine to begin loading and displaying a web page at the given address. It returns immediately even though the actual loading may take some time (if it finishes at all).

We need to make one more change to the program. Add this line to AndroidManifest.xml before the <application> tag:

`BrowserView/AndroidManifest.xml`

```
<uses-permission android:name="android.permission.INTERNET" />
```

If you leave this out, Android will not give your application access to the Internet, and you'll get a "Web page not available" error.

Try running the program now, and enter a valid web address starting with "http://"; when you press Enter or select the Go button, the web page should appear (see Figure 7.3, on the next page).

WebView has dozens of other methods you can use to control what is being displayed or get notifications on state changes.

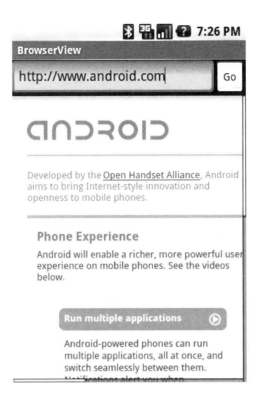

Figure 7.3: EMBEDDING A BROWSER USING WEBVIEW

You can find a complete list in the online documentation for WebView, but here are the methods you are most likely to need:

- addJavascriptInterface(): Allows a Java object to be accessed from JavaScript (more on this one in the next section)
- createSnapshot(): Creates a screenshot of the current page
- getSettings(): Returns a WebSettings object used to control the settings
- loadData(): Loads the given string data into the browser
- loadDataWithBaseURL(): Loads the given data using a base URL
- loadUrl(): Loads a web page from the given URL
- setDownloadListener(): Registers callbacks for download events, such as when the user downloads a .zip or .apk file
- setWebChromeClient(): Registers callbacks for events that need to be done outside the WebView rectangle, such as updating the title or progress bar or opening a JavaScript dialog box

---

\\//
๖ **Joe Asks. . .**
ک
<u>Why Didn't BrowserIntent Need <uses-permission>?</u>

The previous example, BrowserIntent, simply fired off an intent to request that some other application view the web page. That other application (the browser) is the one that needs to ask for Internet permissions in its own AndroidManifest.xml.

- setWebViewClient(): Lets the application set hooks in the browser to intercept events such as resource loads, key presses, and authorization requests
- stopLoading(): Stops the current page from loading

One of the most powerful things you can do with the WebView control is to talk back and forth between it and the Android application that contains it. Let's take a closer look at this feature now.

7.3 From JavaScript to Java and Back

Your Android device can do a number of cool things such as store local data, draw graphics, play music, make calls, and determine its location. Wouldn't it be nice if you could access that functionality from a web page? With an embedded WebView control, you can.

The key is the addJavascriptInterface() method in the WebView class. You can use it to extend the Document Object Model (DOM) inside the embedded browser and to define a new object that JavaScript code can access. When the JavaScript code invokes methods on that object, it will actually be invoking methods in your Android program.

You can call JavaScript methods from your Android program too. All you have to do is call the loadUrl() method, passing it a URL of the form **javascript:**code-to-execute. Instead of going to a new page, the browser will execute the given JavaScript expression inside the current page. You can call a method, change JavaScript variables, modify the browser document—anything you need.

To demonstrate calls between JavaScript in the WebView and Java in the Android program, let us now build a program that is half HTML/

Joe Asks...

Is Allowing JavaScript to Call Java Dangerous?

Whenever you allow a web page to access local resources or call functions outside the browser sandbox, you need to consider the security implications very carefully. For example, you wouldn't want to create a method to allow JavaScript to read data from any arbitrary path name because that might expose some private data to a malicious site that knew about your method and your filenames.

Here are a few things to keep in mind. First, don't rely on security by obscurity. Enforce limits on the pages that can use your methods and on the things those methods can do. And remember the golden rule of security: *don't rule things out; rule them in*. In other words, don't try to check for all the bad things that someone can ask you to do (for example, invalid characters in a query). You're bound to miss something. Instead, disallow everything, and pass only the good things you know are safe.

JavaScript and half Android (see Figure 7.4, on the following page). The top part of the application window is a WebView control, and the bottom part is a TextView and Button from the Android user interface. When you click the buttons and links, it makes calls between the two environments.

Start by creating a "Hello, Android" program using these parameters:

```
Project name: LocalBrowser
Package name: org.example.localbrowser
Activity name: LocalBrowser
Application name: LocalBrowser
```

The user interface for this program will be split into two parts. The first part is defined in the Android layout file, res/layout/main.xml:

LocalBrowser/res/layout/main.xml

```xml
<?xml version="1.0" encoding="utf-8"?>
<LinearLayout
    xmlns:android="http://schemas.android.com/apk/res/android"
    android:orientation="vertical"
    android:layout_width="fill_parent"
    android:layout_height="fill_parent">
```

Figure 7.4: COMMUNICATING BETWEEN ANDROID AND AN EMBEDDED WEBVIEW

```
<WebView
    android:id="@+id/web_view"
    android:layout_width="fill_parent"
    android:layout_height="fill_parent"
    android:layout_weight="1.0" />
<LinearLayout
    android:orientation="vertical"
    android:layout_width="fill_parent"
    android:layout_height="fill_parent"
    android:layout_weight="1.0"
    android:padding="5sp">
    <TextView
        android:layout_width="fill_parent"
        android:layout_height="wrap_content"
        android:textSize="24sp"
        android:text="TextView" />
    <Button
        android:id="@+id/button"
```

```
        android:text="@string/call_javascript_from_android"
        android:layout_width="wrap_content"
        android:layout_height="wrap_content"
        android:textSize="18sp" />
    <TextView
        android:id="@+id/text_view"
        android:layout_width="fill_parent"
        android:layout_height="wrap_content"
        android:textSize="18sp" />
</LinearLayout>
</LinearLayout>
```

The second part is the index.html file that will be loaded into the Web-View. This file goes in the assets directory, not the res directory, because it's not a compiled resource. Anything in the assets directory is copied verbatim onto local storage when your program is installed. The directory is intended to be used for local copies of HTML, images, and scripts that the browser can view without being connected to the network.

LocalBrowser/assets/index.html

```
Line 1  <html>
   -    <head>
   -    <script language="JavaScript">
   -        function callJS(arg) {
   5            document.getElementById('replaceme').innerHTML = arg;
   -        }
   -    </script>
   -    </head>
   -    <body>
   10   <h1>WebView</h1>
   -    <p>
   -    <a href="#" onclick="window.alert('Alert from JavaScript')">
   -        Display JavaScript alert</a>
   -    </p>
   15   <p>
   -    <a href="#" onclick="window.android.callAndroid('Hello from Browser')">
   -        Call Android from JavaScript</a>
   -    </p>
   -    <p id="replaceme">
   20   </p>
   -    </body>
   -    </html>
```

Line 4 of index.html defines the callJS() function that our Android program will be calling later. It takes a string argument and inserts it at the *replaceme* tag, which is at line 19.

In Figure 7.4, on page 128, you see two HTML links that are defined starting at line 12. The first one just calls a standard window.alert() function to open a window displaying a short message. The second link, at line 16, calls the callAndroid() method on the window.android object. If you loaded this page into a normal web browser, window.android would be undefined. But since we're embedding a browser into an Android application, we can define the object ourselves so the page can use it.

Next we turn to the Android code in the LocalBrowser class. Here's the basic outline:

LocalBrowser/src/org/example/localbrowser/LocalBrowser.java

```
Line 1   package org.example.localbrowser;

         import android.app.Activity;
         import android.os.Bundle;
    5    import android.os.Handler;
         import android.util.Log;
         import android.view.View;
         import android.view.View.OnClickListener;
         import android.webkit.JsResult;
   10    import android.webkit.WebChromeClient;
         import android.webkit.WebView;
         import android.widget.Button;
         import android.widget.TextView;
         import android.widget.Toast;
   15
         public class LocalBrowser extends Activity {
             private static final String TAG = "LocalBrowser";
             private final Handler handler = new Handler();
             private WebView webView;
   20        private TextView textView;
             private Button button;

             @Override
             public void onCreate(Bundle savedInstanceState) {
   25            super.onCreate(savedInstanceState);
                 setContentView(R.layout.main);

                 // Find the Android controls on the screen
                 webView = (WebView) findViewById(R.id.web_view);
   30            textView = (TextView) findViewById(R.id.text_view);
                 button = (Button) findViewById(R.id.button);
                 // Rest of onCreate follows...
             }
         }
```

Note the initialization of a Handler object at line 18. JavaScript calls come in on a special thread dedicated to the browser, but Android user interface calls can be made only from the main (GUI) thread. We'll use the Handler class to make the transition.

To call Android Java code from JavaScript, you need to define a plain old Java object with one or more methods, like this:

LocalBrowser/src/org/example/localbrowser/LocalBrowser.java

```
/** Object exposed to JavaScript */
private class AndroidBridge {
    public void callAndroid(final String arg) { // must be final
        handler.post(new Runnable() {
            public void run() {
                Log.d(TAG, "callAndroid(" + arg + ")");
                textView.setText(arg);
            }
        });
    }
}
```

When JavaScript calls the callAndroid() method, the application creates a new Runnable object and post it on the running queue of the main thread using Handler.post(). As soon as the main thread gets a chance, it will invoke the run() method, which will call setText() to change the text on the TextView object.

Now it's time to tie everything together in the onCreate() method. First we turn on JavaScript (it's off by default) and register our bridge to JavaScript:

LocalBrowser/src/org/example/localbrowser/LocalBrowser.java

```
// Turn on JavaScript in the embedded browser
webView.getSettings().setJavaScriptEnabled(true);

// Expose a Java object to JavaScript in the browser
webView.addJavascriptInterface(new AndroidBridge(),
        "android");
```

Then we create an anonymous WebChromeClient object and register it with the setWebChromeClient() method.

LocalBrowser/src/org/example/localbrowser/LocalBrowser.java

```
// Set up a function to be called when JavaScript tries
// to open an alert window
webView.setWebChromeClient(new WebChromeClient() {
    @Override
    public boolean onJsAlert(final WebView view,
            final String url, final String message,
            JsResult result) {
        Log.d(TAG, "onJsAlert(" + view + ", " + url + ", "
            + message + ", " + result + ")");
        Toast.makeText(LocalBrowser.this, message, 3000).show();
        return false;
    }
});
```

The term *chrome* here refers to all the trimmings around a browser window. If this were a full-blown browser client, we'd need to handle navigation, bookmarks, menus, and so forth. In this case, all we want to do is change what happens with JavaScript code when the browser tries to open a JavaScript alert (using window.alert()). Inside onJsAlert() we use the Android Toast class to create a message window that will appear for a short amount of time (in this case, 3000 milliseconds, or 3 seconds).

Once we finish configuring the WebView, we can use loadUrl() to load the local web page:

LocalBrowser/src/org/example/localbrowser/LocalBrowser.java

```
// Load the web page from a local asset
webView.loadUrl("file:///android_asset/index.html");
```

URLs of the form "file:///android_asset/*filename*" (note the three forward slashes) have a special meaning to Android's browser engine. As you might have guessed, they refer to files in the assets directory. In this case, we're loading the index.html file defined earlier.

The last thing we have to do is wire up the button at the bottom of the screen so it will make a JavaScript call (a call from Java to JavaScript).

LocalBrowser/src/org/example/localbrowser/LocalBrowser.java

```
// This function will be called when the user presses the
// button on the Android side
button.setOnClickListener(new OnClickListener() {
    public void onClick(View view) {
        Log.d(TAG, "onClick(" + view + ")");
        webView.loadUrl("javascript:callJS('Hello from Android')");
    }
});
```

To do that, we set a listener for button clicks using setOnClickListener(). When the button is pressed, onClick() is called, which turns around and calls WebView.loadUrl(), passing it a JavaScript expression to evaluate in the browser. The expression is a call to the callJS() function defined in index.html.

Run the program now, and try it. When you click "Display JavaScript alert," an Android message window will appear. When you click "Call Android from JavaScript," the string "Hello from Browser" will be displayed in an Android text control. And finally, when you press the "Call JavaScript from Android" button, the string "Hello from Android" is sent to the browser and inserted in the HTML where it will be displayed at the end of the web page.

Sometimes you don't need to display a web page, but you just need to access some kind of web service or other server-side resource. In the next section, I'll show you how to do this.

7.4 Using Web Services

Android provides a full set of Java-standard networking APIs, such as the java.net.HttpURLConnection package, that you can use in your programs. The tricky part is to make the calls asynchronously so that your program's user interface will be responsive at all times.

Consider what would happen if you just make a blocking network call in your main (GUI) thread. Until that call returns (and it might never return), your application cannot respond to any user interface events such as keystrokes or button presses. It will appear hung to the user. Obviously, that's something you'll have to avoid.

The java.util.concurrent package is perfect for this kind of work. First created by Doug Lea as a stand-alone library and later incorporated into Java 5, this package supports concurrent programming at a higher level than the regular Java Thread class. The ExecutorService class manages one or more threads for you, and all you have to do is submit tasks (instances of Runnable or Callable) to the executor to have them run. An instance of the Future class is returned, which is a reference to some as-yet-unknown future value that will be returned by your task (if any). You can limit the number of threads that are created, and you can interrupt running tasks if necessary.

Figure 7.5: MACHINE TRANSLATION IS STILL A WORK IN PROGRESS.

To illustrate these concepts, let's create a fun little program that calls the Google Translation API.[4] Have you ever laughed at strange translations to and from foreign languages, especially computer-generated translations? This program will let the user enter a phrase in one language, ask Google to translate to a second language, and then ask Google to translate it back into the first language. Ideally, you'd end up with the same words you started with, but this is not always the case, as you can see in Figure 7.5.

To use this program, simply select the starting and target languages, and then start typing a phrase. As you type, the program will use the Google Translation web service to translate your text into and out of the target language.

---

4. http://code.google.com/apis/ajaxlanguage

Lost in Translation

When I first thought of this example, I imagined that it would be easy to get some hilarious results. Unfortunately (or fortunately, depending on your point of view), the Google service does a pretty good job, especially with Romance languages like English and French. If you find any especially funny cases where the translator really flubs up, please post them on the discussion forum at the book's website (http://pragprog.com/titles/eband) for others to enjoy.

To create this application, start with a "Hello, Android" application using these parameters:

```
Project name: Translate
Package name: org.example.translate
Activity name: Translate
Application name: Translate
```

Since this example will access the Internet to make a web service call, we will need to tell Android to grant us permission. Add this line to AndroidManifest.xml after the *<application>* XML tag:

Translate/AndroidManifest.xml

```
<uses-permission android:name="android.permission.INTERNET" />
```

The layout for this example is a little more complicated than usual, so we'll use the TableLayout view. TableLayout lets you arrange your views into rows and columns, taking care of alignment and stretching the columns to fit the content. It's similar to using *<table>* and *<tr>* tags in HTML.

Translate/res/layout/main.xml

```
<?xml version="1.0" encoding="utf-8"?>
<ScrollView
    xmlns:android="http://schemas.android.com/apk/res/android"
    android:layout_width="fill_parent"
    android:layout_height="fill_parent">
    <TableLayout
        android:layout_width="fill_parent"
        android:layout_height="fill_parent"
        android:stretchColumns="1"
        android:padding="10dip">
```

```
    <TableRow>
      <TextView android:text="@string/from_text" />
      <Spinner android:id="@+id/from_language" />
    </TableRow>
    <EditText
      android:id="@+id/original_text"
      android:hint="@string/original_hint"
      android:padding="10dip"
      android:textSize="18sp" />
    <TableRow>
      <TextView android:text="@string/to_text" />
      <Spinner android:id="@+id/to_language" />
    </TableRow>
    <TextView
      android:id="@+id/translated_text"
      android:padding="10dip"
      android:textSize="18sp" />
    <TextView android:text="@string/back_text" />
    <TextView
      android:id="@+id/retranslated_text"
      android:padding="10dip"
      android:textSize="18sp" />
  </TableLayout>
</ScrollView>
```

In this example, we have five rows, each row containing one or two columns. Note that if there is only one view in a row, you don't have to use a TableRow to contain it. Also, it's not necessary to use android: layout_width= and android:layout_height= on every view like you have to with LinearLayout.

The Spinner class is a new one we haven't seen before. It's similar to a combo box in other user interface toolkits. The user selects the spinner (for example, by touching it), and a list of possible values appears for them to pick.[5] In this example, we're going to use this control for selecting from a list of languages.

The actual list is stored as an Android resource in the file res/values/arrays.xml:

`Translate/res/values/arrays.xml`

```
<?xml version="1.0" encoding="utf-8"?>
<resources>
  <array name="languages">
    <item>Bulgarian (bg)</item>
    <item>Chinese Simplified (zh-CN)</item>
```

---

5. In early versions of the SDK, the user could also cycle (spin) through all the values using the arrows or D-pad buttons. However, as of 0.9_beta, Google decided to take that out, leaving the class a bit awkwardly named.

```
<item>Chinese Traditional (zh-TW)</item>
<item>Catalan (ca)</item>
<item>Croatian (hr)</item>
<item>Czech (cs)</item>
<item>Danish (da)</item>
<item>Dutch (nl)</item>
<item>English (en)</item>
<item>Filipino (tl)</item>
<item>Finnish (fi)</item>
<item>French (fr)</item>
<item>German (de)</item>
<item>Greek (el)</item>
<item>Indonesian (id)</item>
<item>Italian (it)</item>
<item>Japanese (ja)</item>
<item>Korean (ko)</item>
<item>Latvian (lv)</item>
<item>Lithuanian (lt)</item>
<item>Norwegian (no)</item>
<item>Polish (pl)</item>
<item>Portuguese (pt-PT)</item>
<item>Romanian (ro)</item>
<item>Russian (ru)</item>
<item>Spanish (es)</item>
<item>Serbian (sr)</item>
<item>Slovak (sk)</item>
<item>Slovenian (sl)</item>
<item>Swedish (sv)</item>
<item>Ukrainian (uk)</item>
    </array>
</resources>
```

This defines a list called languages that contains most of the languages recognized by the Google Translation API. Note that each value has a long name (for example, *Spanish*) and a short name (for example, *es*). We'll use the short name when passing the language to the translator.

Now let's start modifying the Translate class. Here's the basic outline:

Translate/src/org/example/translate/Translate.java

```
Line 1  package org.example.translate;

        import java.util.concurrent.ExecutorService;
        import java.util.concurrent.Executors;
    5   import java.util.concurrent.Future;
        import java.util.concurrent.RejectedExecutionException;

        import android.app.Activity;
        import android.os.Bundle;
   10   import android.os.Handler;
        import android.text.Editable;
        import android.text.TextWatcher;
```

```
 -   import android.view.View;
 -   import android.widget.AdapterView;
15   import android.widget.ArrayAdapter;
 -   import android.widget.EditText;
 -   import android.widget.Spinner;
 -   import android.widget.TextView;
 -   import android.widget.AdapterView.OnItemSelectedListener;
20
 -   public class Translate extends Activity {
 -       private Spinner fromSpinner;
 -       private Spinner toSpinner;
 -       private EditText origText;
25       private TextView transText;
 -       private TextView retransText;
 -
 -       private TextWatcher textWatcher;
 -       private OnItemSelectedListener itemListener;
30
 -       private Handler guiThread;
 -       private ExecutorService transThread;
 -       private Runnable updateTask;
 -       private Future transPending;
35
 -       @Override
 -       public void onCreate(Bundle savedInstanceState) {
 -           super.onCreate(savedInstanceState);
 -
40           setContentView(R.layout.main);
 -           initThreading();
 -           findViews();
 -           setAdapters();
 -           setListeners();
45       }
 -   }
```

After declaring a few variables, we define the onCreate() method starting at line 37 to initialize the threading and user interface. Don't worry, we'll fill out all those other methods it calls as we go.

The findViews() method, called from line 42, just gets a handle to all the user interface elements defined in the layout file:

Translate/src/org/example/translate/Translate.java

```
/** Get a handle to all user interface elements */
private void findViews() {
    fromSpinner = (Spinner) this.findViewById(R.id.from_language);
    toSpinner = (Spinner) this.findViewById(R.id.to_language);
    origText = (EditText) this.findViewById(R.id.original_text);
    transText = (TextView) this.findViewById(R.id.translated_text);
    retransText = (TextView) this.findViewById(R.id.retranslated_text);
}
```

The setAdapters() method, called from onCreate() on line 43, defines a data source for the spinners:

`Translate/src/org/example/translate/Translate.java`

```java
/** Define data source for the spinners */
private void setAdapters() {
   // Spinner list comes from a resource,
   // Spinner user interface uses standard layouts
   ArrayAdapter<CharSequence> adapter = ArrayAdapter.createFromResource(
         this, R.array.languages,
         android.R.layout.simple_spinner_item);
   adapter.setDropDownViewResource(
         android.R.layout.simple_spinner_dropdown_item);
   fromSpinner.setAdapter(adapter);
   toSpinner.setAdapter(adapter);

   // Automatically select two spinner items
   fromSpinner.setSelection(8); // English (en)
   toSpinner.setSelection(11); // French (fr)
}
```

In Android, an Adapter is a class that binds a data source (in this case, the languages array defined in arrays.xml) to a user interface control (in this case, a spinner). We use the standard layouts provided by Android for individual items in the list and for the drop-down box you see when you select the spinner.

Next we set up the user interface handlers in the setListeners() routine (called from line 44 of onCreate()):

`Translate/src/org/example/translate/Translate.java`

```java
/** Setup user interface event handlers */
private void setListeners() {
   // Define event listeners
   textWatcher = new TextWatcher() {
      public void beforeTextChanged(CharSequence s, int start,
            int count, int after) {
         /* Do nothing */
      }
      public void onTextChanged(CharSequence s, int start,
            int before, int count) {
         queueUpdate(1000 /* milliseconds */);
      }
      public void afterTextChanged(Editable s) {
         /* Do nothing */
      }
   };
   itemListener = new OnItemSelectedListener() {
      public void onItemSelected(AdapterView parent, View v,
            int position, long id) {
         queueUpdate(200 /* milliseconds */);
      }
```

\\/ **Joe Asks...**
ٍ؟⁻
___**Is All This Delay and Threading Stuff Really Necessary?**___

One reason you need to do it this way is to avoid making too many calls to the external web service. Imagine what happens as the user enters the word *scissors*. The program sees the word typed in a character at a time, first *s*, then *c*, then *i*, and so on, possibly with backspaces because nobody can remember how to spell *scissors*. Do you really want to make a web service request for every character? Not really. Besides putting unnecessary load on the server, it would be wasteful in terms of power. Each request requires the device's radio to transmit and receive several data packets, which uses up a bit of battery power. You want to wait until the user finishes typing before sending the request, but how do you tell they are done?

The algorithm used here is that as soon as the user types a letter, a delayed request is started. If they don't type another letter before the one-second delay is up, then the request goes through. Otherwise, the first request is removed from the request queue before it goes out. If the request is already in progress, we try to interrupt it. The same goes for language changes, except we use a smaller delay. The good news is that now that I've done it once for you, you can use the same pattern in your own asynchronous programs.

```
    public void onNothingSelected(AdapterView parent) {
        /* Do nothing */
    }
};

// Set listeners on graphical user interface widgets
origText.addTextChangedListener(textWatcher);
fromSpinner.setOnItemSelectedListener(itemListener);
toSpinner.setOnItemSelectedListener(itemListener);
}
```

We define two listeners: one that is called when the text to translate is changed and one that is called when the language is changed. queue-Update() puts a delayed update request on the main thread's to-do list using a Handler. We arbitrarily use a 1,000-millisecond delay for text changes and a 200-millisecond delay for language changes.

The update request is defined inside the initThreading() method:

```
Translate/src/org/example/translate/Translate.java
```

```
Line 1   /**
    -     * Initialize multi-threading. There are two threads: 1) The main
    -     * graphical user interface thread already started by Android,
    -     * and 2) The translate thread, which we start using an executor.
    5     */
    -    private void initThreading() {
    -        guiThread = new Handler();
    -        transThread = Executors.newSingleThreadExecutor();
    -
   10        // This task does a translation and updates the screen
    -        updateTask = new Runnable() {
    -            public void run() {
    -                // Get text to translate
    -                String original = origText.getText().toString().trim();
   15
    -                // Cancel previous translation if there was one
    -                if (transPending != null)
    -                    transPending.cancel(true);
    -
   20                // Take care of the easy case
    -                if (original.length() == 0) {
    -                    transText.setText(R.string.empty);
    -                    retransText.setText(R.string.empty);
    -                } else {
   25                    // Let user know we're doing something
    -                    transText.setText(R.string.translating);
    -                    retransText.setText(R.string.translating);
    -
    -                    // Begin translation now but don't wait for it
   30                    try {
    -                        TranslateTask translateTask = new TranslateTask(
    -                                Translate.this, // reference to activity
    -                                original, // original text
    -                                getLang(fromSpinner), // from language
   35                                getLang(toSpinner) // to language
    -                        );
    -                        transPending = transThread.submit(translateTask);
    -                    } catch (RejectedExecutionException e) {
    -                        // Unable to start new task
   40                        transText.setText(R.string.translation_error);
    -                        retransText.setText(R.string.translation_error);
    -                    }
    -                }
    -            }
   45        };
    -    }
```

We have two threads: the main Android thread used for the user interface and a translate thread that we'll create for running the actual
translation job. We represent the first one with an Android Handler and
the second with Java's ExecutorService.

Line 11 defines the update task, which will be scheduled by the queue-
Update() method. When it gets to run, it first fetches the current text to
translate and then prepares to send a translation job to the translate
thread. It cancels any translation that is already in progress (on line
18), takes care of the case where there is no text to translate (line 22),
and fills in the two text controls where translated text will appear with
the string "Translating..." (line 26). That text will be replaced later by
the actual translated text.

Finally, on line 31, we create an instance of TranslateTask, giving it a
reference to the Translate activity so it can call back to change the text,
a string containing the original text, and the short names of the two
languages selected in the spinners. Line 37 submits the new task to the
translation thread, returning a reference to the Future return value. In
this case, we don't really have a return value since TranslateTask changes
the GUI directly, but we use the Future reference back on line 18 to
cancel the translation if necessary.

To finish up the Translate class, here are a few utility functions used in
other places:

Translate/src/org/example/translate/Translate.java

```java
/** Extract the language code from the current spinner item */
private String getLang(Spinner spinner) {
    String result = spinner.getSelectedItem().toString();
    int lparen = result.indexOf('(');
    int rparen = result.indexOf(')');
    result = result.substring(lparen + 1, rparen);
    return result;
}


/** Request an update to start after a short delay */
private void queueUpdate(long delayMillis) {
    // Cancel previous update if it hasn't started yet
    guiThread.removeCallbacks(updateTask);
    // Start an update if nothing happens after a few milliseconds
    guiThread.postDelayed(updateTask, delayMillis);
}


/** Modify text on the screen (called from another thread) */
public void setTranslated(String text) {
    guiSetText(transText, text);
}
```

```
/** Modify text on the screen (called from another thread) */
public void setRetranslated(String text) {
    guiSetText(retransText, text);
}

/** All changes to the GUI must be done in the GUI thread */
private void guiSetText(final TextView view, final String text) {
    guiThread.post(new Runnable() {
        public void run() {
            view.setText(text);
        }
    });
}
```

The getLang() method figures out which item is currently selected in a spinner, gets the string for that item, and parses out the short language code needed by the Translation API.

queueUpdate() puts an update request on the main thread's request queue but tells it to wait a little while before actually running it. If there was already a request on the queue, it's removed.

The setTranslated() and setRetranslated() methods will be used by TranslateTask to update the user interface when translated results come back from the web service. They both call a private function called guiSetText().

guiSetText() uses the Handler.post() method to ask the main GUI thread to update the text on a TextView control. This extra step is necessary because you can't call user interface functions from non-user-interface threads, and guiSetText() will be called by the translate thread.

Here is the res/values/strings.xml file for the Translate example:

Translate/res/values/strings.xml

```
<?xml version="1.0" encoding="utf-8"?>
<resources>
    <string name="app_name">Translate</string>
    <string name="from_text">From:</string>
    <string name="to_text">To:</string>
    <string name="back_text">And back again:</string>
    <string name="original_hint">Enter text to translate</string>
    <string name="empty"></string>
    <string name="translating">Translating...</string>
    <string name="translation_error">(Translation error)</string>
    <string name="translation_interrupted">(Translation
        interrupted)</string>
</resources>
```

I'm not going to include the source to the TranslateTask class here because it's rather long and contains nothing Android specific except for a few debugging messages. If you'd like to see a nice example of calling a RESTful web service using HttpURLConnection, parsing results in Java-Script Object Notation (JSON) format, and handling all sorts of network errors and requests for interruptions, then you can download the source from the book's website.

7.5 Fast-Forward >>

In this chapter, we covered a lot of ground, from opening a simple web page to using an asynchronous web service. HTML/JavaScript programming is beyond the scope of this book, but there are several good references available. If you're going to do much concurrent programming with classes such as ExecutorService, I recommend *Java Concurrency in Practice* [Goe06] by Brian Goetz.

The next chapter will explore a new level of interactivity through location and sensor services. If you're anxious to learn more about data sources and data binding, you can skip ahead to Chapter 9, *Putting SQL to Work*, on page 161.

Locating and Sensing

The Android platform uses many different technologies. Some of them are new, and some have been seen before in other settings. What's unique about Android is how these technologies work together. In this chapter, we'll consider the following:

- Location awareness, through inexpensive GPS devices

- Handheld accelerometers, such as those found on the Nintendo Wii remote

- Mashups, often combining maps with other information

Several of the winners of the Android Developer's Challenge[1] used these concepts to create a more compelling and relevant experience for the user. For example, the Locale application[2] can adapt the settings on your phone based on where you are. Are you always forgetting to set your ringer to vibrate when you're at work or the movies? Locale can take care of that using the Android Location API described here.

8.1 Location, Location, Location

Right now there are 31 satellites zipping around the world with nothing better to do than help you find your way to the grocery store. The Global Positioning System (GPS), originally developed by the military but then converted to civilian use, beams highly precise time signals to Earth-based receivers such as the one in your Android phone. With

---

1. http://code.google.com/android/adc_gallery/index.html
2. http://www.androidlocale.com

> \\//
> ⁻⁆⁅ **Joe Asks...**
> ⁻⁀
> **Does GPS Let Anyone Snoop on My Location?**
>
> No. GPS receivers are just that—receivers. The GPS chip, and thus any program running in your Android device, knows where it is. But unless one of those programs deliberately transmits that information, nobody can use it to find you.

good reception and a little math, the GPS chip can figure out your position to within 50 feet.[3]

In addition to GPS, Android also supports calculating your position using information from nearby cell phone towers, and if you're connected to a wifi hotspot, it can use that too. Keep in mind that all these location providers are unreliable to some extent. When you walk inside a building, for example, GPS signals can't reach you.

To demonstrate Android's location services, let's write a test program that simply displays your current position and keeps updating it on the screen as you move around. You can see the program in Figure 8.1, on the facing page.

Where Am I?

Start by creating a "Hello, Android" application using these parameters in the New Project wizard:

```
Project name: LocationTest
Package name: org.example.locationtest
Activity name: LocationTest
Application name: LocationTest
```

Access to location information is protected by Android permissions. To gain access, you'll need to add these lines in the AndroidManifest.xml file before the <*application*> tag:

LocationTest/AndroidManifest.xml
```
<uses-permission android:name="android.permission.ACCESS_COARSE_LOCATION" />
<uses-permission android:name="android.permission.ACCESS_FINE_LOCATION" />
```

---

3. You don't have to know how GPS works to use it, but if you're curious, see http://adventure.howstuffworks.com/gps.htm.

Figure 8.1: TESTING THE LOCATIONMANAGER

In this example, both fine-grained location providers such as GPS and course-grained location providers such as cell tower triangulation will be supported.

For the user interface, we're going to print all the location data into a big scrolling TextView, which is defined in res/layout/main.xml:

LocationTest/res/layout/main.xml

```xml
<?xml version="1.0" encoding="utf-8"?>
<ScrollView
    xmlns:android="http://schemas.android.com/apk/res/android"
    android:orientation="vertical"
    android:layout_width="fill_parent"
    android:layout_height="fill_parent">
    <TextView
        android:id="@+id/output"
        android:layout_width="fill_parent"
        android:layout_height="wrap_content" />
</ScrollView>
```

With the preliminaries out of the way, we can start coding. Here's the outline of the LocationTest class and the onCreate() method. (Ignore the reference to LocationListener on line 15 for now; we'll come back to it later.)

```
LocationTest/src/org/example/locationtest/LocationTest.java
Line 1  package org.example.locationtest;

        import java.util.List;

     5  import android.app.Activity;
        import android.location.Criteria;
        import android.location.Location;
        import android.location.LocationListener;
        import android.location.LocationManager;
    10  import android.location.LocationProvider;
        import android.os.Bundle;
        import android.widget.TextView;

        public class LocationTest extends Activity implements
    15          LocationListener {
          private LocationManager mgr;
          private TextView output;
          private String best;

    20    @Override
          public void onCreate(Bundle savedInstanceState) {
            super.onCreate(savedInstanceState);
            setContentView(R.layout.main);

    25      mgr = (LocationManager) getSystemService(LOCATION_SERVICE);
            output = (TextView) findViewById(R.id.output);

            log("Location providers:");
            dumpProviders();
    30
            Criteria criteria = new Criteria();
            best = mgr.getBestProvider(criteria, true);
            log("\nBest provider is: " + best);

    35      log("\nLocations (starting with last known):");
            Location location = mgr.getLastKnownLocation(best);
            dumpLocation(location);
          }
        }
```

The starting point for Android location services is the getSystemService() call on line 25. It returns a LocationManager class that we save into a field for later use.

On line 29, we call our dumpProviders() method to print a list of all the location providers in the system.

Next we need to pick one of the possible providers to use. I've seen some examples that simply pick the first available one, but I recommend using the getBestProvider() method, as shown here. Android will pick the best provider according to a Criteria that you provide (see line 31). If you have any restrictions on cost, power, accuracy, and so on, this is where you put them. In this example, there are no restrictions.

Depending on the provider, it may take some time for the device to figure out your current location. This could be a few seconds, a minute, or more. However, Android remembers the last position it returned, so we can query and print that immediately on line 36. This location could be out of date—for example, if the device was turned off and moved— but it's usually better than nothing.

Knowing where we were is only half the fun. Where are we going next?

Updating the Location

To have Android notify you about location changes, call the requestLocationUpdates() method on the LocationManager object. To save battery power, we want updates only when the program is in the foreground. Therefore, we need to hook into the Android activity life-cycle methods by overriding onResume() and onPause():

LocationTest/src/org/example/locationtest/LocationTest.java

```
@Override
protected void onResume() {
    super.onResume();
    // Start updates (doc recommends delay >= 60000 ms)
    mgr.requestLocationUpdates(best, 15000, 1, this);
}

@Override
protected void onPause() {
    super.onPause();
    // Stop updates to save power while app paused
    mgr.removeUpdates(this);
}
```

When the application resumes, we call requestLocationUpdates() to start the update process. It takes four parameters: the provider name, a delay (so you don't get updates too often), a minimum distance (changes less than this are ignored), and a LocationListener object.

When the application pauses, we call removeUpdates() to stop getting updates. The location provider will be powered down if it's not needed for a while.

Now you know why LocationTest implements LocationListener, so we could just pass a reference to the activity instead of making a new listener object. That will save us about 1KB of memory at runtime.

Here's the definition of the four methods required by that interface:

`LocationTest/src/org/example/locationtest/LocationTest.java`

```
public void onLocationChanged(Location location) {
    dumpLocation(location);
}

public void onProviderDisabled(String provider) {
    log("\nProvider disabled: " + provider);
}

public void onProviderEnabled(String provider) {
    log("\nProvider enabled: " + provider);
}

public void onStatusChanged(String provider, int status,
        Bundle extras) {
    log("\nProvider status changed: " + provider + ", status="
        + S[status] + ", extras=" + extras);
}
```

The most important method in the bunch is onLocationChanged().

As the name suggests, it's called every time the provider notices that the device's location has changed. The onProviderDisabled(), onProviderEnabled(), and onStatusChanged() methods can be used to switch to other providers in case your first choice becomes unavailable.

The code for the remaining methods of LocationTest—log(), dumpProviders(), and dumpLocation()—is not very interesting, so I won't bore you with it here. You can find it all in the downloadable samples on the book's website.

Emulation Notes

If you run the LocationTest example on a real device, it will show your current position as you walk around. On the emulator, it uses a fake GPS provider that always returns the same position unless you change it. Let's do that now.

In Eclipse you can change your simulated location using the Emulator Control view (Window > Show View > Other... > Android > Emulator Control). Scroll down to the bottom, and you'll find a place to enter the longitude and latitude manually. When you click the Send button, Eclipse will send the new position to the emulated device, and you'll see it displayed in any programs that are watching for it.

You can also run the DDMS program outside of Eclipse and send fake position changes in that way. In addition to manual, position-at-a-time updates, you can use a recorded path read from an external file. See the DDMS documentation for more information.[4]

With Android location providers, you can find out where you are in a broad, global sense. If you want more local information such as tilt and temperature, you have to use a different API. That's the subject of the next section.

8.2 Set Sensors to Maximum

Let's say you're writing a racing game so you need to give the player a way to steer their car on the screen. One way would be to use buttons, like driving games on a Sony Playstation or the Nintendo DS. Press right to steer right, press left to steer left, and hold down another button for the gas. It works, but it's not very natural.

Have you ever watched somebody play one of those games? Unconsciously, they sway from side to side when making a hairpin curve, jerk the controller when bumping into another car, lean forward when speeding up, and pull back when putting on the breaks. Wouldn't it be cool if those motions actually had some effect on the game play? Now they can.

Engaging Sensors

The Android SDK supports many different types of sensor devices:

- SENSOR_ACCELEROMETER: Measures acceleration in the x, y, and z axes
- SENSOR_LIGHT: Tells you how bright your surrounding area is
- SENSOR_MAGNETIC_FIELD: Returns magnetic attraction in the x, y, and z axes

---

4. http://code.google.com/android/reference/ddms.html

- SENSOR_ORIENTATION: Measures the yaw, pitch, and roll of the device
- SENSOR_ORIENTATION_RAW: Same thing as SENSOR_ORIENTATION without filtering
- SENSOR_PROXIMITY: Provides the distance between the sensor and some object
- SENSOR_TEMPERATURE: Measures the temperature of the surrounding area
- SENSOR_TRICORDER: Turns your device into a fully functional Star Trek Tricorder[5]

Not all devices will offer all this functionality, of course.

Android's SensorManager class is similar to LocationManager, except the updates will come much more quickly, perhaps hundreds per second. To get access to the sensors, you first call the getSystemService() method like this:

SensorTest/src/org/example/sensortest/SensorTest.java

```
private SensorManager mgr;
    // ...
    mgr = (SensorManager) getSystemService(SENSOR_SERVICE);
```

Then you call the registerListener() in your onResume() method to start getting updates and unregisterListener() in your onPause() method to stop getting them.

Interpreting Sensor Readings

The sensor service will call your onSensorChanged() method every time a value changes. It should look something like this:

SensorTest/src/org/example/sensortest/SensorTest.java

```
public void onSensorChanged(int sensor, float[] values) {
    for (int i = 0; i < values.length; i++) {
        // ...
    }
}
```

All the sensors return an array of floating-point values. The size of the array depends on the particular sensor; for example, SENSOR_ TEMPERATURE returns only one value, the temperature in degrees Celsius. You may not even need to use all the numbers returned. For

---

5. Darn it, Jim—I'm a programmer, not an *ovum paschalis*.

instance, if you just need a compass heading, you can use the first number returned from the SENSOR_ORIENTATION sensor.

Turning the sensor readings (especially from the accelerometer) into meaningful information is something of a black art. Here are a few tips to keep in mind:

- Accelerometer readings are extremely jittery. You'll need to smooth out the data using some kind of weighted averaging, but you have to be careful not to smooth it too much, or your interface will feel laggy and soft.

- Sensor numbers will come in at random times. You may get several in a row, then have a short pause, and then receive a bunch more. Don't assume a nice even rate.

- Try to get ahead of the user by predicting what they're going to do next. Let's say the last three readings show the start of a roll to the right, with each one a little faster than the last. You can guess with some degree of accuracy what the next reading is going to be and start reacting based on your prediction.

The most challenging use of sensors is an action game that requires a one-to-one connection between how the player moves the device and what happens on the screen. Unfortunately, the emulator isn't going to be much use for this kind of thing.

Emulation Notes

According to Google, it is not possible to test the sensors using the emulator at all. Most computers don't have a light sensor, a GPS chip, or a compass built into them. Sure enough, if you run the SensorTest program (available from the book's website) in the emulator, it will display no results at all. However, a project called OpenIntents[6] provides an alternate sensor's API that you can call just for testing purposes.

The way it works is that you connect the emulator to another application running on your desktop computer called the Sensor Simulator. The simulator shows a picture of a virtual phone and lets you move it around on the screen with the mouse (see Figure 8.2, on the next page), and then it feeds those movements to your Android program running on the emulator. If your development computer actually does have sensors of its own (like the Apple MacBook) or you can connect to a Wii

---

6. http://www.openintents.org

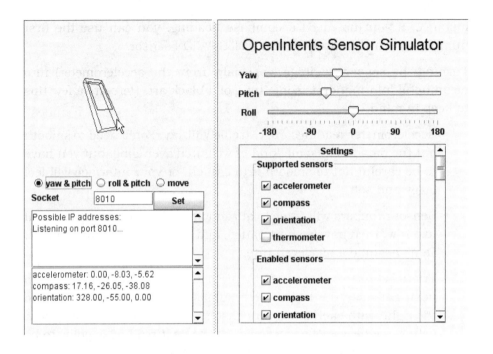

Figure 8.2: FAKING OUT THE SENSORS WITH THE SENSOR SIMULATOR

remote with Bluetooth, the Sensor Simulator can use that as a data source.

The downside is that you have to modify your source code to make it work. See the OpenIntents website for more information if you want to try it. My recommendation is to forget about sensor emulation and get your hands on a real device. Keep tweaking your algorithms until it feels right.

Now that you know the low-level calls to get your location and query the sensors for numbers such as your compass heading, for certain applications you can forget all that and just use the Google Maps API.

8.3 Bird's-Eye View

One of the first "killer apps" for Ajax was Google Maps.[7] Using Java-Script and the XmlHttpRequest object, Google engineers created a drag-

---

7. http://maps.google.com

gable, zoomable, silky-smooth map viewer that ran in any modern web browser without a plug-in. The idea was quickly copied by other vendors such as Microsoft and Yahoo, but the Google version is arguably still the best.

You can use these web-based maps in Android, perhaps with an embedded WebView control as discussed in Section 7.2, *Web with a View*, on page 121. But the architecture of your application would be overly convoluted. That's why Google created the MapView control.

Embedding a MapView

A MapView can be embedded directly in your Android application with just a few lines of code. Most of the functionality of Google Maps, plus hooks for adding your own touches, is provided (see Figure 8.3, on the next page).

The MapView class can also tie into your location and sensor providers. It can show your current location on the map and even display a compass showing what direction you're heading. Let's create a sample program to demonstrate a few of its capabilities.

First create a "Hello, Android" application using these values in the wizard:

```
Project name: MyMap
Package name: org.example.mymap
Activity name: MyMap
Application name: MyMap
```

Edit the layout file, and replace it with a MapView that takes over the whole screen:

MyMap/res/layout/main.xml

```
<?xml version="1.0" encoding="utf-8"?>
<FrameLayout
    xmlns:android="http://schemas.android.com/apk/res/android"
    android:id="@+id/frame"
    android:orientation="vertical"
    android:layout_width="fill_parent"
    android:layout_height="fill_parent">
    <com.google.android.maps.MapView
        android:id="@+id/map"
        android:apiKey="MapAPIKey"
        android:layout_width="fill_parent"
        android:layout_height="fill_parent"
        android:clickable="true" />
</FrameLayout>
```

Figure 8.3: EMBEDDED MAP SHOWING YOUR CURRENT LOCATION

We use a FrameLayout here so we can stick the zoom controls on top of the map later. Substitute *MapAPIKey* with a Google Maps API key that you get from Google.[8]

Note that we have to use the fully qualified name (com.google.android. maps.MapView) because MapView is not a standard Android class. We also need to stick a *<uses-library>* tag in the *<application>* element of AndroidManifest.xml.

MyMap/AndroidManifest.xml

```
<?xml version="1.0" encoding="utf-8"?>
<manifest xmlns:android="http://schemas.android.com/apk/res/android"
    package="org.example.mymap"
    android:versionCode="1"
    android:versionName="1.0.0">
  <uses-permission
        android:name="android.permission.ACCESS_COARSE_LOCATION" />
```

---

8. http://code.google.com/android/maps-api-signup.html

```
        <uses-permission
            android:name="android.permission.ACCESS_FINE_LOCATION" />
        <uses-permission
            android:name="android.permission.INTERNET" />
        <application android:icon="@drawable/icon"
            android:label="@string/app_name">
          <uses-library android:name="com.google.android.maps" />
          <activity android:name=".MyMap"
                android:label="@string/app_name">
            <intent-filter>
                <action android:name="android.intent.action.MAIN" />
                <category android:name="android.intent.category.LAUNCHER" />
            </intent-filter>
          </activity>
        </application>
</manifest>
```

If you leave out the <uses-library> tag, you will get a runtime error
saying that the MapView class was not found.

In addition to the fine- and coarse-grained location providers, the Map-
View class needs Internet access so that it can call Google's servers
to get the map image tiles. These will be cached in your application
directory automatically.

Here's the outline of the MyMap class:

MyMap/src/org/example/mymap/MyMap.java

```java
package org.example.mymap;

import android.os.Bundle;
import android.view.Gravity;
import android.view.View;
import android.view.ViewGroup.LayoutParams;
import android.widget.FrameLayout;

import com.google.android.maps.MapActivity;
import com.google.android.maps.MapController;
import com.google.android.maps.MapView;
import com.google.android.maps.MyLocationOverlay;

public class MyMap extends MapActivity {
    private FrameLayout frame;
    private MapView map;
    private MapController controller;

    @Override
    public void onCreate(Bundle savedInstanceState) {
        super.onCreate(savedInstanceState);
        setContentView(R.layout.main);
```

```
            initMapView();
            initZoomControls();
            initMyLocation();
        }
        @Override
        protected boolean isRouteDisplayed() {
            // Required by MapActivity
            return false;
        }
    }
```

The most important part is that your activity has to extend MapActivity. The MapActivity class spins up the background threads, connects to the Internet for tile data, handles caching, does animations, takes care of the life cycle, and much more. All you need to do is properly set it up and let it go.

Getting Ready

The first thing we need to do is call findViewById() to get access to the MapView and its container. We can do that in the initMapView() method:

MyMap/src/org/example/mymap/MyMap.java

```
/** Find and initialize the map view. */
private void initMapView() {
    frame = (FrameLayout) findViewById(R.id.frame);
    map = (MapView) findViewById(R.id.map);
    controller = map.getController();
    map.setSatellite(true);
}
```

The getController() method returns a MapController that we'll use to position and zoom the map.

Speaking of zooming, we need to create and position the zoom controls in the initZoomControls() method.

MyMap/src/org/example/mymap/MyMap.java

```
/** Get the zoom controls and add them to the bottom of the map. */
private void initZoomControls() {
    View zoomControls = map.getZoomControls();
    FrameLayout.LayoutParams p = new FrameLayout.LayoutParams(
        LayoutParams.WRAP_CONTENT, LayoutParams.WRAP_CONTENT,
        Gravity.BOTTOM + Gravity.CENTER_HORIZONTAL);
    frame.addView(zoomControls, p);
}
```

The MapView class handles everything about the zoom controls except where they go on the screen. All we need to do is get a handle to them and add them to our parent frame using a layout that centers the controls at the bottom of the screen. MapView will take care of making the controls visible when the user pans the map and fading them out slowly when panning stops.

The last step is to tell the MapView to follow your position in the initMy-Location() method:

MyMap/src/org/example/mymap/MyMap.java

```
/** Start tracking the position on the map. */
private void initMyLocation() {
    final MyLocationOverlay overlay = new MyLocationOverlay(this, map);
    overlay.enableMyLocation();
    overlay.enableCompass(); // no effect in emulator
    overlay.runOnFirstFix(new Runnable() {
        public void run() {
            // Zoom in to current location
            controller.setZoom(8);
            controller.animateTo(overlay.getMyLocation());
        }
    });
    map.getOverlays().add(overlay);
}
```

Android provides a MyLocationOverlay class that does most of the heavy lifting. An overlay is just something that is drawn on top of the map, which in this case is a pulsing dot showing your current location. You call enableMyLocation() to tell the overlay to start listening to location updates and enableCompass() to tell it to start listening to updates from the compass.

The runOnFirstFix() method tells the overlay what to do the first time it gets a position reading from the location provider. In this case, we set the zoom level and then start an animation that moves the map from wherever it's pointing now to where you are located.

If you run the program now, you should see something like Figure 8.3, on page 156. Touch and drag the screen to move around the map, and use the zoom buttons to get a closer look. When you walk around carrying the phone, the dot on the map should follow you.

Emulation Notes

If you run the program on the emulator instead of a real device, you'll initially see a zoomed-out map of the world and no dot for your current location. As before, use the Emulator Control view in Eclipse (or in the stand-alone DDMS program) to feed fake GPS data to the sample application. When running in the emulator, the compass inset will not be shown because the compass sensor is not emulated.

8.4 Fast-Forward >>

This chapter introduced you to the exciting new world of location- and environmental-aware mobile computing. These technologies, in combination with trends such as the adoption of broadband mobile Internet and the exponential growth of computing power and storage, are going to revolutionize the way we interact with computers and with each other.

Another way to perceive the world is by looking and listening. Android provides the Camera class[9] for taking photographs using the built-in camera (if there is one), but you can also use it to do other things like make a bar-code reader. The MediaRecorder class[10] allows you to record and store audio clips. These are beyond the scope of this book, but if you need them for your program, consult the online documentation.

Speaking of storage, the next chapter will show you how to use SQL to store structured information (for example, a travel log of locations, photographs, and notes) locally on your mobile phone. If that's not your area of interest, you can skip ahead to Chapter 10, *3D Graphics in OpenGL*, on page 181 and learn how to unlock Android's hidden 3D graphics potential.

---

9. http://code.google.com/android/reference/android/hardware/Camera.html
10. http://code.google.com/android/reference/android/media/MediaRecorder.html

Chapter 9

Putting SQL to Work

In Chapter 6, *Storing Local Data*, on page 105, we explored keeping data around in Preferences and in plain files. That works fine when the amount of data is small or when the data is all one type (such as a picture or an audio file). However, there is a better way to store large amounts of structured data: a relational database.

For the past 30 years, databases have been a staple of enterprise application development, but until recently they were too expensive and unwieldy for smaller-scale use. That is changing with small embedded engines such as the one included with the Android platform.

This chapter will show you how to use Android's embedded database engine, SQLite. You'll also learn how to use Android's data binding to connect your data sources to your user interface. Finally, you'll look at the ContentProvider class, which allows two applications to share the same data.

9.1 Introducing SQLite

SQLite[1] is a tiny yet powerful database engine created by Dr. Richard Hipp in 2000. It is arguably the most widely deployed SQL database engine in the world. Besides Android, SQLite can be found in the Apple iPhone, Symbian phones, Mozilla Firefox, Skype, PHP, Adobe AIR, Mac OS X, Solaris, and many other places.

---

1. http://www.sqlite.org

SQLite License

The SQLite source code contains no license because it is in the public domain. Instead of a license, the source offers you this blessing:

May you do good and not evil.

May you find forgiveness for yourself and forgive others.

May you share freely, never taking more than you give.

There are three reasons why it is so popular:

- It's free. The authors have placed it in the public domain and don't charge for its use.
- It's small. The current version is about 150KB, well within the memory budget of an Android phone.
- It requires no setup or administration. There is no server, no config file, and no need for a database administrator.

A SQLite database is just a file. You can take that file, move it around, and even copy it to another system (for example, from your phone to your workstation), and it will work fine. Android stores the file in the /data/data/*packagename*/databases directory (see Figure 9.1, on the next page). You can use the adb command or the File Explorer view in Eclipse (Window > Show View > Other... > Android > File Explorer) to view, move, or delete it.

Instead of calling Java I/O routines to access this file from your program, you run Structured Query Language (SQL) statements. Through its helper classes and convenience methods, Android hides some of the syntax from you, but you still need to know a bit of SQL to use it.

9.2 SQL 101

If you've used Oracle, SQL Server, MySQL, DB2, or other database engines, then SQL should be old hat to you. You can skip this section and go to Section 9.3, *Hello, Database*, on page 164. For the rest of you, here's a quick refresher.

To use a SQL database, you submit SQL statements and get back results. There are three main types of SQL statements: DDL, Modification, and Query.

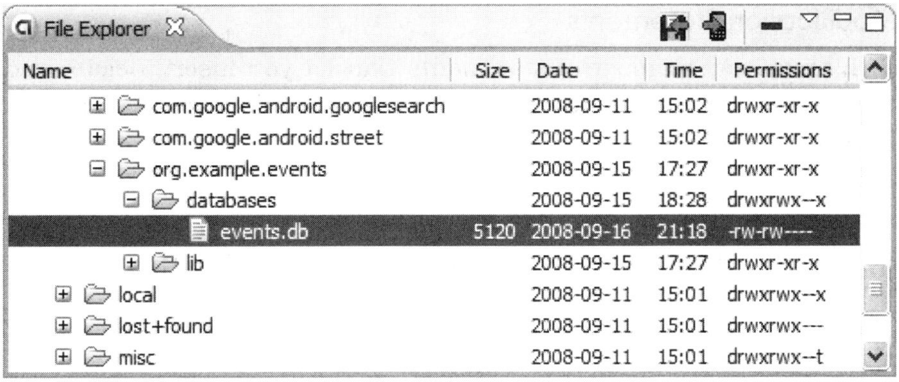

Figure 9.1: SQLite STORES AN ENTIRE DATABASE IN ONE FILE.

DDL Statements

A database file can have any number of tables. A table consists of rows, and each row has a certain number of columns. Each column of the table has a name and a data type (text string, number, and so forth). You define these tables and column names by first running Data Definition Language (DDL) statements. Here's a statement that creates a table with three columns:

SQLite/create.sql

```
create table mytable (
    _id integer primary key autoincrement,
    name text,
    phone text );
```

One of the columns is designated as the **PRIMARY KEY**, a number that uniquely identifies the row. **AUTOINCREMENT** means that the database will add 1 to the key for every record to make sure it's unique. By convention, the first column is always called _id. The _id column isn't strictly required for SQLite, but later when we want to use an Android ContentProvider, we'll need it.

Note that, unlike most databases, in SQLite the column types are just hints. If you try to store a string in an integer column, or vice versa, it will just work with no complaints. The SQLite authors consider this to be a feature, not a bug.

Modification Statements

SQL provides a number of statements that let you insert, delete, and update records in the database. For example, to add a few phone numbers, you could use this:

SQLite/insert.sql

```
insert into mytable values(null, 'Steven King', '555-1212');
insert into mytable values(null, 'John Smith', '555-2345');
insert into mytable values(null, 'Fred Smitheizen', '555-4321');
```

The values are specified in the same order you used in the **CREATE TABLE** statement. We specify **NULL** for _id because SQLite will figure that value out for us.

Query Statements

Once data has been loaded into a table, you run queries against the table using a **SELECT** statement. For example, if you wanted to get the third entry, you could do this:

SQLite/selectid.sql

```
select * from mytable where(_id=3);
```

It's more likely you'd want to do a look up a person's phone number by name. Here's how you'd find all the records containing "Smith" in the name:

SQLite/selectwhere.sql

```
select name, phone from mytable where(name like "%smith%");
```

Keep in mind that SQL is case insensitive. Keywords, column names, and even search strings can be specified in either uppercase or lowercase.

Now you know just enough about SQL to be dangerous. Let's see how to put that knowledge to work in a simple program.

9.3 Hello, Database

To demonstrate SQLite, let's create a little application called Events that stores records in a database and displays them later. We're going to start simple and build up from there. Open a new "Hello, Android" program using these values in the project wizard:

```
Project name: Events
Package name: org.example.events
Activity name: Events
Application name: Events
```

As always, you can download the complete source code from the book's website.

We need somewhere to hold a few constants describing the database, so let's create a Constants interface:

Eventsv1/src/org/example/events/Constants.java

```java
package org.example.events;

import android.provider.BaseColumns;

public interface Constants extends BaseColumns {
    public static final String TABLE_NAME = "events";

    // Columns in the Events database
    public static final String TIME = "time";
    public static final String TITLE = "title";
}
```

Each event will be stored as a row in the events table. Each row will have an _id, time, and title column. _id is the primary key, declared in the BaseColumns interface that we extend. time and title will be used for a time stamp and event title, respectively.

Using SQLiteOpenHelper

Next we create a helper class called EventsData to represent the database itself. This class extends the Android SQLiteOpenHelper class, which manages database creation and versions. All you need to do is provide a constructor and override two methods.

Eventsv1/src/org/example/events/EventsData.java

```java
package org.example.events;

import static android.provider.BaseColumns._ID;
import static org.example.events.Constants.TABLE_NAME;
import static org.example.events.Constants.TIME;
import static org.example.events.Constants.TITLE;
import android.content.Context;
import android.database.sqlite.SQLiteDatabase;
import android.database.sqlite.SQLiteOpenHelper;

public class EventsData extends SQLiteOpenHelper {
    private static final String DATABASE_NAME = "events.db";
    private static final int DATABASE_VERSION = 1;

    /** Create a helper object for the Events database */
    public EventsData(Context ctx) {
        super(ctx, DATABASE_NAME, null, DATABASE_VERSION);
    }
```

Joe Asks...

Why Is Constants an Interface?

It's a Java thing. I don't know about you, but I dislike having to repeat the class name every time I use a constant. For example, I want to just type TIME and not Constants.TIME. Traditionally, the way to do that in Java is use interfaces. Classes can inherit from the Constants interface and then leave out the interface name when referencing any fields. If you look at the BaseColumns interface, you'll see the Android programmers used the same trick.

Starting with Java 5, however, there's a better way: static imports. That's the method I'll use in EventsData and other classes in this chapter. Since Constants is an interface, you can use it the old way or the new way as you prefer.

Unfortunately, as of this writing, Eclipse's support for static imports is a little spotty, so if you use static imports in your own programs, Eclipse may not insert the import statements for you automatically. Here's a little trick for Eclipse users: type a wildcard static import after the package statement (for example, import static org.example.events.Constants.*;) to make things compile. Later, you can use Source > Organize Imports to expand the wildcard and sort the import statements. Let's hope this will be more intuitive in future versions of Eclipse.

```
20    @Override
      public void onCreate(SQLiteDatabase db) {
          db.execSQL("CREATE TABLE " + TABLE_NAME + " (" + _ID
              + " INTEGER PRIMARY KEY AUTOINCREMENT, " + TIME
              + " INTEGER," + TITLE + " TEXT NOT NULL);");
25    }

      @Override
      public void onUpgrade(SQLiteDatabase db, int oldVersion,
          int newVersion) {
30        db.execSQL("DROP TABLE IF EXISTS " + TABLE_NAME);
          onCreate(db);
      }
    }
```

The constructor starts on line 16. DATABASE_NAME is the actual filename of the database we'll be using (events.db), and DATABASE_VERSION is just a number we make up. If this were a real program, you would increase the version number whenever you had to make significant changes to the database design (for example, to add a new column).

The first time you try to access a database, SQLiteOpenHelper will notice it doesn't exist and call the onCreate() method to create it. On line 21, we override that and run a **CREATE TABLE** SQL statement. This will create the events table and the events.db database file that contains it.

When Android detects you're referencing an old database (based on the version number), it will call the onUpgrade() method (line 28). In this example, we just delete the old table, but you could do something smarter here if you like. For example, you could run an **ALTER TABLE** SQL command to add a column to an existing database.

Defining the Main Program

Our first attempt at the Events program will use a local SQLite database to store the events, and it will show them as a string inside a TextView. Define the layout file (layout/main.xml) as follows:

Eventsv1/res/layout/main.xml

```xml
<?xml version="1.0" encoding="utf-8"?>
<ScrollView
    xmlns:android="http://schemas.android.com/apk/res/android"
    android:layout_width="fill_parent"
    android:layout_height="fill_parent">
    <TextView
        android:id="@+id/text"
        android:layout_width="fill_parent"
        android:layout_height="wrap_content" />
</ScrollView>
```

This declares the TextView with an imaginative ID of text (R.id.text in code) and wraps it with a ScrollView in case there are too many events to fit on the screen. You can see how it looks in Figure 9.2, on the next page.

The main program is the onCreate() method in the Events activity.

Figure 9.2: THE FIRST VERSION DISPLAYS DATABASE RECORDS IN A
TEXTVIEW.

Here's the outline:

Eventsv1/src/org/example/events/Events.java

```
Line 1  package org.example.events;

        import static android.provider.BaseColumns._ID;
        import static org.example.events.Constants.TABLE_NAME;
5       import static org.example.events.Constants.TIME;
        import static org.example.events.Constants.TITLE;
        import android.app.Activity;
        import android.content.ContentValues;
        import android.database.Cursor;
10      import android.database.sqlite.SQLiteDatabase;
        import android.os.Bundle;
        import android.widget.TextView;

        public class Events extends Activity {
15          private EventsData events;

            @Override
            public void onCreate(Bundle savedInstanceState) {
                super.onCreate(savedInstanceState);
20              setContentView(R.layout.main);
                events = new EventsData(this);
                try {
                    addEvent("Hello, Android!");
                    Cursor cursor = getEvents();
25                  showEvents(cursor);
                } finally {
                    events.close();
                }
            }
30      }
```

On line 20 of onCreate(), we set the layout for this view. Then we create an instance of the EventsData class on line 21 and start a **try** block. If you look ahead to line 27, you can see we close the database inside the **finally** block. So even if an error occurs in the middle, the database will still be closed.

The events table wouldn't be very interesting if there weren't any events, so on line 23 we call the addEvent() method to add an event to it. Every time you run this program, you'll get a new event. You could add menus or gestures or keystrokes to generate other events if you like, but I'll leave that as an exercise to the reader.

On line 24, we call the getEvents() method to get the list of events, and finally on line 25, we call the showEvents() method to display the list to the user.

Pretty easy, eh? Now let's define those new methods we just used.

Adding a Row

The addEvent() method cuts a new record in the database using the string provided as the event title.

Eventsv1/src/org/example/events/Events.java

```
private void addEvent(String string) {
    // Insert a new record into the Events data source.
    // You would do something similar for delete and update.
    SQLiteDatabase db = events.getWritableDatabase();
    ContentValues values = new ContentValues();
    values.put(TIME, System.currentTimeMillis());
    values.put(TITLE, string);
    db.insertOrThrow(TABLE_NAME, null, values);
}
```

Since we need to modify the data, we call getWritableDatabase() to get a read/write handle to the events database. The database handle is cached, so you can call this method as many times as you like.

Next we fill in a ContentValues object with the current time and the event title and pass that to the insertOrThrow() method to do the actual **INSERT** SQL statement. You don't need to pass in the record ID because SQLite will make one up and return it from the method call.

As the name implies, insertOrThrow() can throw an exception (of type SQLException) if it fails. It doesn't have to be declared with a **throws** keyword because it's a RuntimeException and not a checked exception. However, if you want to, you can still handle it in a **try/catch** block like any other exception. If you don't handle it and there is an error, the program will terminate, and a traceback will be dumped to the Android log.

By default, as soon as you do the insert, the database is updated. If you need to batch up or delay modifications for some reason, consult the SQLite website for more details.

Running a Query

The getEvents() method does the database query to get a list of events:

Eventsv1/src/org/example/events/Events.java
```
private static String[] FROM = { _ID, TIME, TITLE, };
private static String ORDER_BY = TIME + " DESC";
private Cursor getEvents() {
    // Perform a managed query. The Activity will handle closing
    // and re-querying the cursor when needed.
    SQLiteDatabase db = events.getReadableDatabase();
    Cursor cursor = db.query(TABLE_NAME, FROM, null, null, null,
            null, ORDER_BY);
    startManagingCursor(cursor);
    return cursor;
}
```

We don't need to modify the database for a query, so we call getReadableDatabase() to get a read-only handle. Then we call query() to perform the actual **SELECT** SQL statement. FROM is an array of the columns we want, and ORDER_BY tells SQLite to return the results in order from newest to oldest.

Although we don't use them in this example, the query() method has parameters to specify a **WHERE** clause, a **GROUP BY** clause, and a **HAVING** clause. Actually, query() is just a convenience for the programmer. If you prefer, you could build up the **SELECT** statement yourself in a string and use the rawQuery() method to execute it. Either way, the return value is a Cursor object that represents the result set.

A Cursor is similar to a Java Iterator or a JDBC ResultSet. You call methods on it to get information about the current row, and then you call another method to move to the next row. We'll see how to use it when we display the results in a moment.

The final step is to call startManagingCursor(), which tells the activity to take care of managing the cursor's life cycle based on the activity's life cycle. For example, when the activity is paused, it will automatically deactivate the cursor and then requery it when the activity is restarted. When the activity terminates, all managed cursors will be closed.

Displaying the Query Results

The last method we need to define is showEvents(). This function takes a Cursor as input and formats the output so the user can read it.

`Eventsv1/src/org/example/events/Events.java`

```
Line 1    private void showEvents(Cursor cursor) {
    -         // Stuff them all into a big string
    -         StringBuilder builder = new StringBuilder(
    -             "Saved events:\n");
    5         while (cursor.moveToNext()) {
    -             // Could use getColumnIndexOrThrow() to get indexes
    -             long id = cursor.getLong(0);
    -             long time = cursor.getLong(1);
    -             String title = cursor.getString(2);
    10            builder.append(id).append(": ");
    -             builder.append(time).append(": ");
    -             builder.append(title).append("\n");
    -         }
    -         // Display on the screen
    15        TextView text = (TextView) findViewById(R.id.text);
    -         text.setText(builder);
    -     }
```

In this version of Events, we're just going to create a big string (see line 3) to hold all the events items, separated by newlines. This is not the recommended way to do things, but it'll work for now.

Line 5 calls the Cursor.moveToNext() method to advance to the next row in the data set. When you first get a Cursor, it is positioned before the first record, so calling moveToNext() gets you to the first record. We keep looping until moveToNext() returns false, which indicates there are no more rows.

Inside the loop (line 7), we call getLong() and getString() to fetch data from the columns of interest, and then we append the values to the string (line 10). There is another method on Cursor, getColumnIndex-OrThrow(), that we could have used to get the column index numbers (the values 0, 1, and 2 passed to getLong() and getString()). However, it's a little slow, so if you need it, you should call it outside the loop and remember the indexes yourself.

Once all the rows have been processed, we look up the TextView from layout/main.xml and stuff the big string into it (line 15).

If you run the example now, you should see something like Figure 9.2, on page 168. Congratulations on your first Android database program! There is plenty of room for improvement, though.

What would happen if there were thousands or millions of events in the list? The program would be very slow and might run out of memory trying to build a string to hold them all. What if you wanted to let the user select one event and do something with it? If everything is in a string, you can't do that. Luckily, Android provides a better way: data binding.

9.4 Data Binding

Data binding allows you to connect your model (data) to your view with just a few lines of code. To demonstrate data binding, we'll modify the Events example to use a ListView that is bound to the result of a database query. First, we need to make the Events class extend ListActivity instead of Activity:

Eventsv2/src/org/example/events/Events.java
```
public class Events extends ListActivity {
    // ...
}
```

Next, we need to change how the events are displayed in the Events. showEvents() method:

Eventsv2/src/org/example/events/Events.java
```
private static int[] TO = { R.id.rowid, R.id.time, R.id.title, };
private void showEvents(Cursor cursor) {
    // Set up data binding
    SimpleCursorAdapter adapter = new SimpleCursorAdapter(this,
        R.layout.item, cursor, FROM, TO);
    setListAdapter(adapter);
}
```

Notice this code is much smaller than before (two lines vs. ten). The first line creates a SimpleCursorAdapter for the Cursor, and the second line tells the ListActivity to use the new adapter. The adapter acts as a go-between, connecting the view with its data source.

If you recall, we first used an adapter in the Translate sample program (see Translate.setAdapters() in Section 7.4, *Using Web Services*, on page 133). In that example, we used an ArrayAdapter because the data source was an array defined in XML. For this one, we use a SimpleCursorAdapter because the data source is a Cursor object that came from a database query.

The constructor for SimpleCursorAdapter takes five parameters:

- *context*: A reference to the current Activity
- *layout*: A resource that defines the views for a single list item
- *cursor*: The data set cursor
- *from*: The list of column names where the data is coming from
- *to*: The list of views where the data is going to

The layout for a list item is defined in layout/item.xml. Note the definitions for the row ID, time, and title views that are referenced in the TO array.

Eventsv2/res/layout/item.xml

```xml
<?xml version="1.0" encoding="utf-8"?>
<RelativeLayout
    xmlns:android="http://schemas.android.com/apk/res/android"
    android:layout_width="fill_parent"
    android:layout_height="fill_parent"
    android:orientation="horizontal"
    android:padding="10sp">
    <TextView
        android:id="@+id/rowid"
        android:layout_width="wrap_content"
        android:layout_height="wrap_content" />
    <TextView
        android:id="@+id/rowidcolon"
        android:layout_width="wrap_content"
        android:layout_height="wrap_content"
        android:text=": "
        android:layout_toRightOf="@id/rowid" />
    <TextView
        android:id="@+id/time"
        android:layout_width="wrap_content"
        android:layout_height="wrap_content"
        android:layout_toRightOf="@id/rowidcolon" />
    <TextView
        android:id="@+id/timecolon"
        android:layout_width="wrap_content"
        android:layout_height="wrap_content"
        android:text=": "
        android:layout_toRightOf="@id/time" />
    <TextView
        android:id="@+id/title"
        android:layout_width="fill_parent"
        android:layout_height="wrap_content"
        android:ellipsize="end"
        android:singleLine="true"
        android:textStyle="italic"
        android:layout_toRightOf="@id/timecolon" />
</RelativeLayout>
```

This looks more complicated than it is. All we're doing is putting the ID, time, and title on one line with colons in between the fields. I added a little padding and formatting to make it look nice.

Finally, we need to change the layout for the activity itself in layout/main.xml. Here's the new version:

```
Eventsv2/res/layout/main.xml
<?xml version="1.0" encoding="utf-8"?>
<LinearLayout
    xmlns:android="http://schemas.android.com/apk/res/android"
    android:layout_width="fill_parent"
    android:layout_height="fill_parent">
    <!-- Note built-in ids for 'list' and 'empty' -->
    <ListView
        android:id="@android:id/list"
        android:layout_width="wrap_content"
        android:layout_height="wrap_content"/>
    <TextView
        android:id="@android:id/empty"
        android:layout_width="wrap_content"
        android:layout_height="wrap_content"
        android:text="@string/empty" />
</LinearLayout>
```

Because the activity extends ListActivity, Android looks for two special IDs in the layout file. If the list has items in it, the android:id/list view will be displayed; otherwise, the android:id/empty view will be displayed. So if there are no items, instead of a blank screen the user will see the message "No events!"

For the final result, see Figure 9.3, on the facing page. As an exercise for the reader, think about how you could enhance this application now that you have a real list to play with. For example, when the user selects an event, you could open a detail viewer, mail the event to technical support, or perhaps delete the selected event and all the ones below it from the database.

There's still one little problem with this example. No other application can add things to the events database or even look at them! For that, we'll need to use an Android ContentProvider.

9.5 Using a ContentProvider

In the Android security model (see the discussion above in Section 2.5, *Safe and Secure*, on page 22), files written by one application cannot be

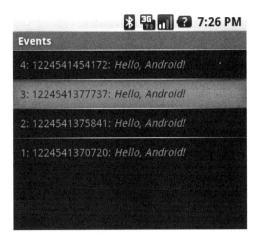

Figure 9.3: THIS VERSION USES A LISTACTIVITY AND DATA BINDING.

read from or written to by any other application. Each program has its own Linux user ID and data directory (/data/data/*packagename*) and its own protected memory space. Android programs can communicate with each other in two ways:

- *Inter-Process Communication (IPC)*: One process declares an arbitrary API using the Android Interface Definition Language (AIDL) and the IBinder interface. Parameters are marshaled safely and efficiently between processes when the API is called. This advanced technique is used for remote procedure calls to a background Service thread.[2]

- *ContentProvider*: Processes register themselves to the system as providers of certain kinds of data. When that information is requested, they are called by Android through a fixed API to query or modify the content in whatever way they see fit. This is the technique we're going to use for the Events sample.

Any piece of information managed by a ContentProvider is addressed through a URI that looks like this:

content://*authority*/*path*/*id*

where:

- content:// is the standard required prefix.
- *authority* is the name of the provider. Using your fully qualified package name is recommended to prevent name collisions.
- *path* is a virtual directory within the provider that identifies the kind of data being requested.
- *id* is the primary key of a specific record being requested. To request all records of a particular type, omit this and the trailing slash.

Android comes with several providers already built in, including the following:[3]

- content://browser
- content://contacts
- content://media
- content://settings

To demonstrate using a ContentProvider, let's convert the Events example to use one. For our Events provider, these will be valid URIs:

```
content://org.example.events/events/3  -- single event with _id=3
content://org.example.events/events  -- all events
```

First we need to add a two more constants to Constants.java:

Eventsv3/src/org/example/events/Constants.java

```
public static final String AUTHORITY = "org.example.events";
public static final Uri CONTENT_URI = Uri.parse("content://"
    + AUTHORITY + "/" + TABLE_NAME);
```

The layout files (main.xml and item.xml) don't need to be changed, so the next step is to make a few minor changes to the Events class.

---

3. For an up-to-date list, see http://code.google.com/android/reference/android/provider/package-summary.html. Instead of using the strings here, use the documented constants such as Browser.BOOKMARKS_URI. Note that access to some providers requires additional permissions to be requested in your manifest file.

Changing the Main Program

The main program (the Events.onCreate() method) actually gets a little simpler because there is no database object to keep track of:

Eventsv3/src/org/example/events/Events.java

```java
@Override
public void onCreate(Bundle savedInstanceState) {
    super.onCreate(savedInstanceState);
    setContentView(R.layout.main);
    addEvent("Hello, Android!");
    Cursor cursor = getEvents();
    showEvents(cursor);
}
```

We don't need the **try/finally** block, and we can remove references to EventData.

Adding a Row

Two lines change in addEvent(). Here's the new version:

Eventsv3/src/org/example/events/Events.java

```java
private void addEvent(String string) {
    // Insert a new record into the Events data source.
    // You would do something similar for delete and update.
    ContentValues values = new ContentValues();
    values.put(TIME, System.currentTimeMillis());
    values.put(TITLE, string);
    getContentResolver().insert(CONTENT_URI, values);
}
```

The call to getWritableDatabase() is gone, and the call to insertOrThrow() is replaced by getContentResolver().insert(). Instead of a database handle, we use a content URI.

Running a Query

The getEvents() method is also simplified when using a ContentProvider:

Eventsv3/src/org/example/events/Events.java

```java
private Cursor getEvents() {
    // Perform a managed query. The Activity will handle closing
    // and re-querying the cursor when needed.
    return managedQuery(CONTENT_URI, FROM, null, null, ORDER_BY);
}
```

Here we use the Activity.managedQuery() method, passing it the content URI, the list of columns we're interested in, and the order they should be sorted in.

By removing all references to the database, we've decoupled the Events client from the Events data provider. The client is simpler, but now we have to implement a new piece we didn't have before.

9.6 Implementing a ContentProvider

A ContentProvider is a high-level object like an Activity that needs to be declared to the system. So, the first step when making one is to add it to your AndroidManifest.xml file before the <*activity*> tag (as a child of <*application*>):

`Eventsv3/AndroidManifest.xml`

```
<provider android:name="EventsProvider"
        android:authorities="org.example.events" />
```

android:name is the class name, and android:authorities is the string used in the content URI.

Next we create the EventsProvider class, which must extend Content-Provider. Here's the basic outline:

`Eventsv3/src/org/example/events/EventsProvider.java`

```
package org.example.events;

import static android.provider.BaseColumns._ID;
import static org.example.events.Constants.AUTHORITY;
import static org.example.events.Constants.CONTENT_URI;
import static org.example.events.Constants.TABLE_NAME;
import android.content.ContentProvider;
import android.content.ContentUris;
import android.content.ContentValues;
import android.content.UriMatcher;
import android.database.Cursor;
import android.database.sqlite.SQLiteDatabase;
import android.net.Uri;
import android.text.TextUtils;

public class EventsProvider extends ContentProvider {
    private static final int EVENTS = 1;
    private static final int EVENTS_ID = 2;

    /** The MIME type of a directory of events */
    private static final String CONTENT_TYPE
        = "vnd.android.cursor.dir/vnd.example.event";

    /** The MIME type of a single event */
    private static final String CONTENT_ITEM_TYPE
        = "vnd.android.cursor.item/vnd.example.event";
```

```
    private EventsData events;
    private UriMatcher uriMatcher;
    // ...
}
```

By convention we use vnd.example instead of org.example in the MIME type.[4] EventsProvider handles two types of data:

- EVENTS (MIME type CONTENT_TYPE): A directory or list of events

- EVENTS_ID (MIME type CONTENT_ITEM_TYPE): A single event

In terms of the URI, the difference is that the first type does not specify an ID, but the second type does. We use Android's UriMatcher class to parse the URI and tell us which one the client specified. And we reuse the EventsData class from earlier in the chapter to manage the real database inside the provider.

In the interest of space, I'm not going to show the rest of the class here, but you can download the whole thing from the book website. All three versions of the Events example can be found in the source code .zip file.

The final version of the Events sample looks exactly like the previous version on the outside (see Figure 9.3, on page 175). On the inside, however, you now have the framework for a event store that can be used by other applications in the system, even ones written by other developers.

9.7 Fast-Forward >>

In this chapter, we learned how to store data in an Android SQL database. If you want to do more with SQL, you'll need to learn about more statements and expressions than the ones we covered here. A book such as *SQL Pocket Guide* [Gen06] by Jonathan Gennick or *The Definitive Guide to SQLite* [Owe06] by Mike Owens would be a good investment, but keep in mind that the SQL syntax and functions vary slightly from database to database.

Another option for data storage on Android is db4o.[5] This library is larger than SQLite and uses a different license (GNU Public License),

---

4. Multipurpose Internet Mail Extensions (MIME) is an Internet standard for describing the type of any kind of content.
5. http://www.db4o.com/android

but it's free and may be easier for you to use, especially if you don't know SQL.

The SimpleCursorAdapter introduced in this chapter can be customized to show more than just text. For example, you could display rating stars or sparklines or other views based on data in the Cursor. Look for ViewBinder in the SimpleCursorAdapter documentation for more information.[6]

And now for something completely different...the next chapter will cover 3D graphics with OpenGL.

---

6. http://code.google.com/android/reference/android/widget/SimpleCursorAdapter.html

3D Graphics in OpenGL

Two-dimensional graphics are great for most programs, but sometimes you need an extra level of depth, interactivity, or realism that isn't possible in 2D. For these times, Android provides a three-dimensional graphics library based on the OpenGL ES standard. In this chapter, we'll explore 3D concepts and build up a sample program that uses OpenGL.

0.1 Understanding 3D Graphics

The world is three-dimensional, yet we routinely view it in two dimensions. When you watch television or look at a picture in a book, the 3D images are flattened out, or *projected*, onto a 2D surface (the TV panel or book page).

Try this simple experiment: cover one eye and look out the window. What do you see? Light from the sun bounces off objects outside, passes through the window, and travels to your eye so you can perceive it. In graphics terms, the scene outside is projected onto the window (or *viewport*). If someone replaced your window with a high-quality photograph, it would look the same until you moved.

Based on how close your eye is to the window and how big the window is, you can see a limited amount of the world outside. This is called your *field of view*. If you draw a line from your eye to the four corners of the window and beyond, you would get the pyramid in Figure 10.1, on the next page. This is called the *view frustum* (Latin for a "piece broken off"). For performance reasons, the frustum is usually bounded by near and far clipping planes as well. You can see everything inside the frustum but nothing outside of it.

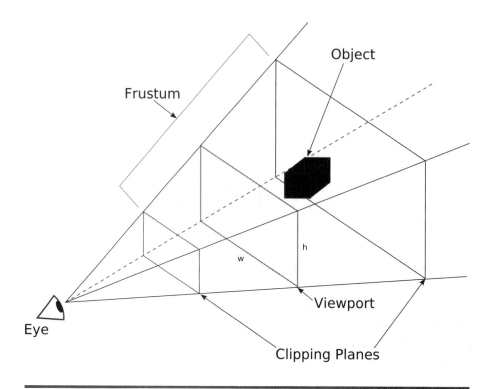

Figure 10.1: VIEWING A THREE-DIMENSIONAL SCENE

In 3D computer graphics, your computer screen acts as the viewport. Your job is to fool the user into thinking it's a window into another world just on the other side of the glass. The OpenGL graphics library is the API you use to accomplish that.

10.2 Introducing OpenGL

OpenGL[1] was developed by Silicon Graphics in 1992. It provides a unified interface for programmers to take advantage of hardware from any manufacturer. At its core, OpenGL implements familiar concepts such as viewports and lighting and tries to hide most of the hardware layer from the developer.

Because it was designed for workstations, OpenGL is too large to fit on a mobile device. So, Android implements a subset of OpenGL called

---

1.   http://www.opengl.org

Thank You, John Carmack

OpenGL has proven to be very successful, but it almost wasn't. In 1995, Microsoft introduced a competitor called Direct3D. Owing to Microsoft's dominant market position and significant R&D investments, for a while it looked like Direct3D was going to take over as a de facto industry standard for gaming. However, one man, John Carmack, cofounder of id Software, refused to comply. His wildly popular Doom and Quake games almost single-handedly forced hardware manufacturers to keep their OpenGL device drivers up-to-date on the PC. Today's Linux, Mac OS X, and mobile device users can thank John and id Software for helping to keep the OpenGL standard relevant.

OpenGL for Embedded Systems (OpenGL ES).[2] This standard was created by the Khronos Group, an industry consortium of companies such as Intel, AMD, Nvidia, Nokia, Samsung, and Sony. The same library (with minor differences) is now available on major mobile platforms including Android, Symbian, and iPhone.

Every language has its own language bindings for OpenGL ES, and Java is no exception. Java's language binding was defined by a Java Specification Request (JSR) 239.[3] Android implements this standard as closely as possible, so you can refer to a variety of books and documentation on JSR 239 and OpenGL ES for a full description of all its classes and methods.

Now let's take a look at how to create a simple OpenGL program in Android.

10.3 Building an OpenGL Program

Begin by creating a new "Hello, Android" project as in Section 1.2, *Creating Your First Program*, on page 6, but this time supply the following parameters in the New Android Project dialog box:

```
Project name: OpenGL
Package name: org.example.opengl
Activity name: OpenGL
Application name: OpenGL
```

---

2. http://www.khronos.org/opengles
3. http://jcp.org/en/jsr/detail?id=239

> ### \\// Joe Asks...
> ### ‿ Will Every Phone Have 3D?
>
> Yes and no. Some low-end devices running Android may not
> actually have 3D hardware. However, the OpenGL program-
> ming interface will still be there. All the 3D functions will be emu-
> lated in software. Your program will still run, but it will be much
> slower than a hardware-accelerated device. For this reason,
> it's a good idea to provide options for users to turn off certain
> details and special effects that take time to draw but aren't
> absolutely necessary for the program. That way, if the user is run-
> ning your program on a slower device, they can disable some
> of your eye candy to get better performance.

This will create OpenGL.java to contain your main activity. Edit this,
and change it to refer to a custom view named GLView, as shown next.
(Remember, you can find the latest version of all this code at http://
pragprog.com/titles/eband, or just click the filename before the code if
you're reading the PDF.)

`OpenGL/src/org/example/opengl/OpenGL.java`

```java
package org.example.opengl;

import android.app.Activity;
import android.os.Bundle;

public class OpenGL extends Activity {
    @Override
    public void onCreate(Bundle savedInstanceState) {
        super.onCreate(savedInstanceState);
        setContentView(new GLView(this));
    }
}
```

We won't need the layout resource (res/layout/main.xml), so you can delete
it. Now let's define our custom view class:

`OpenGL/src/org/example/opengl/GLView.java`

```java
package org.example.opengl;

import android.content.Context;
import android.view.SurfaceHolder;
import android.view.SurfaceView;
```

```
class GLView extends SurfaceView implements SurfaceHolder.Callback {
    GLView(Context context) {
        super(context);

        // Install a SurfaceHolder.Callback so we get notified when
        // the underlying surface is created and destroyed
        getHolder().addCallback(this);

        // Use hardware acceleration if available
        getHolder().setType(SurfaceHolder.SURFACE_TYPE_GPU);
    }

    public void surfaceCreated(SurfaceHolder holder) {
    }

    public void surfaceDestroyed(SurfaceHolder holder) {
    }

    public void surfaceChanged(SurfaceHolder holder, int format,
            int w, int h) {
        // TODO: handle window size changes
    }
}
```

This example introduces several new classes you need to know:

- SurfaceView: A special kind of view that is used for 3D graphics. Extend this for any view that uses OpenGL.
- Surface: A place for drawing, like a Canvas (see Section 4.1, *Canvas*, on page 59), except it is implemented by the 3D hardware (if any). The Surface will be created when your OpenGL activity is running in the foreground and destroyed when the activity exits or some other activity comes to the foreground.
- SurfaceHolder: An instance of this class is always there even if the Surface that it holds goes away.
- SurfaceHolder.Callback: A SurfaceView implements this interface so OpenGL will notify it when the view's Surface is created, destroyed, or resized.

In the next section, we'll fill the screen with a solid color.

10.4 Managing Threads

As we saw in Section 4.2, *Drawing the Board*, on page 66, the Android 2D library calls the onDraw() method of your view whenever it needs to redraw a section of the screen. OpenGL doesn't work that way.

In OpenGL, you create your own thread that is dedicated to drawing the display. Let's do that now:

OpenGL/src/org/example/opengl/GLView.java

```java
private GLThread glThread;

public void surfaceCreated(SurfaceHolder holder) {
    // The Surface has been created so start our drawing thread
    glThread = new GLThread(this);
    glThread.start();
}

public void surfaceDestroyed(SurfaceHolder holder) {
    // Stop our drawing thread. The Surface will be destroyed
    // when we return
    glThread.requestExitAndWait();
    glThread = null;
}
```

In the GLView class, we declare a variable for the thread called glThread with a type of our custom GLThread class. When the OpenGL surface is created, we'll start a new thread to handle its drawing, and when the surface is about to be destroyed, we'll terminate the thread.

Now let's see how the GLThread class is defined. We'll start with this outline:

OpenGL/src/org/example/opengl/GLThread.java

```java
package org.example.opengl;

import javax.microedition.khronos.egl.EGL10;
import javax.microedition.khronos.egl.EGL11;
import javax.microedition.khronos.egl.EGLConfig;
import javax.microedition.khronos.egl.EGLContext;
import javax.microedition.khronos.egl.EGLDisplay;
import javax.microedition.khronos.egl.EGLSurface;
import javax.microedition.khronos.opengles.GL10;

import android.app.Activity;
import android.content.Context;
import android.opengl.GLU;

class GLThread extends Thread {
    private final GLView view;
    private boolean done = false;

    GLThread(GLView view) {
        this.view = view;
    }
```

```
        @Override
        public void run() {
            // Initialize OpenGL...
            // Loop until asked to quit
            while (!done) {
                // Draw a single frame here...
            }
        }

        public void requestExitAndWait() {
            // Tell the thread to quit
            done = true;
            try {
                join();
            } catch (InterruptedException ex) {
                // Ignore
            }
        }
    }
}
```

This is regular Java thread coding—nothing special here. The requestEx-
itAndWait() method is called when the surface is destroyed. Instead of
trying to destroy the thread itself (which is not safe in Java), it simply
sets a flag and waits for the thread to notice and shut itself down. That
shouldn't take more than a fraction of a second.

Now let's fill out the run() method:

OpenGL/src/org/example/opengl/GLThread.java

```
Line 1   @Override
    -    public void run() {
    -        // Initialize OpenGL...
    -        EGL10 egl = (EGL10) EGLContext.getEGL();
    5        EGLDisplay display = egl.eglGetDisplay(EGL10.EGL_DEFAULT_DISPLAY);

    -        int[] version = new int[2];
    -        egl.eglInitialize(display, version);

   10        int[] configSpec = { EGL10.EGL_RED_SIZE, 5,
    -                EGL10.EGL_GREEN_SIZE, 6, EGL10.EGL_BLUE_SIZE, 5,
    -                EGL10.EGL_DEPTH_SIZE, 16, EGL10.EGL_NONE };

    -        EGLConfig[] configs = new EGLConfig[1];
   15        int[] numConfig = new int[1];
    -        egl.eglChooseConfig(display, configSpec, configs, 1,
    -                numConfig);
    -        EGLConfig config = configs[0];

   20        EGLContext glc = egl.eglCreateContext(display, config,
    -                EGL10.EGL_NO_CONTEXT, null);
    -
```

```
      EGLSurface surface = egl.eglCreateWindowSurface(display,
          config, view.getHolder(), null);
25    egl.eglMakeCurrent(display, surface, surface, glc);

      GL10 gl = (GL10) (glc.getGL());
      init(gl);

30    // Loop until asked to quit
      while (!done) {
          // Draw a single frame here...
          drawFrame(gl);
          egl.eglSwapBuffers(display, surface);
35
          // Error handling
          if (egl.eglGetError() == EGL11.EGL_CONTEXT_LOST) {
              Context c = view.getContext();
              if (c instanceof Activity) {
40                ((Activity) c).finish();
              }
          }
      }

45    // Free OpenGL resources
      egl.eglMakeCurrent(display, EGL10.EGL_NO_SURFACE,
          EGL10.EGL_NO_SURFACE, EGL10.EGL_NO_CONTEXT);
      egl.eglDestroySurface(display, surface);
      egl.eglDestroyContext(display, glc);
50    egl.eglTerminate(display);
  }
```

The first thing it needs to do is get a handle to the EGL10 object on line 4. Then we get a Display handle (line 5) and initialize it (line 8), and then we ask OpenGL to find a configuration that matches our particular color depth needs (line 10). I arbitrarily asked for 16-bit color with 5 bits of red, 6 of green, and 5 of blue, but your own application may have other requirements.[4]

With the configuration in hand, we can create the OpenGL context on line 20, create a surface on line 23, and set the current values for display, surface, and context on line 25.

On line 27, we use the getGL() function to return the actual OpenGL interface. We cast it to GL10 so we can call the OpenGL ES 1.0 methods. Although you may notice that Android has a few methods from 1.1

---

4. The Android calls to initialize OpenGL got a lot more complicated in version 0.9_beta. Let's hope in a future version Google will provide some helper functions to simplify it again, but for now just hold your nose and copy the code.

> ## Version 1.what?
>
> OpenGL ES 1.0 is based on full OpenGL version 1.3, and ES 1.1 is based on OpenGL 1.5. JSR 239 has two versions: the original 1.0 and a maintenance release version 1.0.1. There are also some OpenGL ES extensions that I won't get into. Android implements JSR 239 1.0.1, and OpenGL ES implements 1.0. In the future, it's expected that Android will support OpenGL ES 1.1 and beyond.
>
> Don't let all the 1.x versions worry you. These standards have evolved over a period of several years. By now, they are fairly stable and well thought out.

and OpenGL extensions, they are not fully implemented, so you should avoid them for the time being. Besides, everything you're likely to need is already covered by GL10.

After calling the init() method on line 28 to initialize OpenGL options, we start the main loop. The thread will spin here drawing frames continuously until the done flag is true.

OpenGL objects consume a significant amount of resources, so at the end of the run() method starting on line 46, we explicitly destroy them so those resources can be freed.

Now let's take a look at the init() method:

OpenGL/src/org/example/opengl/GLThread.java

```
Line 1   private void init(GL10 gl) {
             // Define the view frustrum
             gl.glViewport(0, 0, view.getWidth(), view.getHeight());
             gl.glMatrixMode(GL10.GL_PROJECTION);
      5      gl.glLoadIdentity();
             float ratio = (float) view.getWidth() / view.getHeight();
             GLU.gluPerspective(gl, 45.0f, ratio, 1, 100f);

             // Set up any other options we need
     10      gl.glEnable(GL10.GL_DEPTH_TEST);
             gl.glDepthFunc(GL10.GL_LEQUAL);
             gl.glEnableClientState(GL10.GL_VERTEX_ARRAY);
             // Optional: disable dither to boost performance
             // gl.glDisable(GL10.GL_DITHER);
     15  }
```

The init() method takes care of setting up our view frustum and a few OpenGL options. Note the call to the GLU.gluPerspective() helper function on line 7. The last two arguments are the distance from the eye to the near and far clipping planes (see Figure 10.1, on page 182).

On line 10, we set a couple of OpenGL options. OpenGL has dozens of options that can be enabled or disabled with glEnable() and glDisable(). The most commonly used ones include the following:

Option	Description
GL_BLEND	Blend the incoming color values with the values already in the color buffer.
GL_CULL_FACE	Ignore polygons based on their winding (clockwise or counterclockwise) in window coordinates. This is a cheap way to eliminate back faces.
GL_DEPTH_TEST	Do depth comparisons, and update the depth buffer. Pixels farther away than those already drawn will be ignored.
GL_LIGHTi	Include light number i when figuring out an object's brightness and color.
GL_LIGHTING	Turn on lighting and material calculations.
GL_LINE_SMOOTH	Draw antialiased lines (lines without jaggies).
GL_MULTISAMPLE	Perform multisampling for antialiasing and other effects.
GL_POINT_SMOOTH	Draw antialiased points.
GL_TEXTURE_2D	Use textures to draw surfaces.

All options are off by default except for GL_DITHER and GL_MULTISAMPLE. Note that everything you enable has some cost in performance.

It's time to draw something. The drawFrame() method is called every time around in the main loop.

OpenGL/src/org/example/opengl/GLThread.java

```java
private void drawFrame(GL10 gl) {
    // Clear the screen to black
    gl.glClear(GL10.GL_COLOR_BUFFER_BIT
        | GL10.GL_DEPTH_BUFFER_BIT);

    // Position model so we can see it
    gl.glMatrixMode(GL10.GL_MODELVIEW);
    gl.glLoadIdentity();
    gl.glTranslatef(0, 0, -3.0f);

    // Other drawing commands go here...
}
```

Figure 10.2: THAT WAS A LOT OF TROUBLE TO GET A BLACK SCREEN.

All we do for now is set the screen to black. We clear both the color and depth buffers. Always remember to clear both, or you'll get some very strange results left over from the depth information for the previous frame.

If you run the program now, you get Figure 10.2. If you're thinking that it's silly to draw the same black screen over and over again in a loop, you're right. However, we'll need the loop later when we talk about animation, so just bear with me for now.

Let's move on and draw something a little more interesting. But first we need to define exactly what we're drawing (the model).

10.5 Building a Model

Depending on the complexity of the objects you want to draw, you will typically create them using a graphical design tool and import them into your program. For the purposes of this example, we'll just define a simple model in code: a cube.

```
Line 1    package org.example.opengl;

          import java.nio.ByteBuffer;
          import java.nio.ByteOrder;
      5   import java.nio.IntBuffer;

          import javax.microedition.khronos.opengles.GL10;

          import android.content.Context;
     10   import android.graphics.Bitmap;
          import android.graphics.BitmapFactory;

          class GLCube {
              private final IntBuffer mVertexBuffer;
     15       public GLCube() {
                  int one = 65536;
                  int half = one / 2;
                  int vertices[] = {
                      // FRONT
     20               -half, -half, half, half, -half, half,
                      -half, half, half, half, half, half,
                      // BACK
                      -half, -half, -half, -half, half, -half,
                      half, -half, -half, half, half, -half,
     25               // LEFT
                      -half, -half, half, -half, half, half,
                      -half, -half, -half, -half, half, -half,
                      // RIGHT
                      half, -half, -half, half, half, -half,
     30               half, -half, half, half, half, half,
                      // TOP
                      -half, half, half, half, half, half,
                      -half, half, -half, half, half, -half,
                      // BOTTOM
     35               -half, -half, half, -half, -half, -half,
                      half, -half, half, half, -half, -half, };
                  // Buffers to be passed to gl*Pointer() functions must be
                  // direct, i.e., they must be placed on the native heap
                  // where the garbage collector cannot move them.
     40           //
                  // Buffers with multi-byte data types (e.g., short, int,
                  // float) must have their byte order set to native order
                  ByteBuffer vbb = ByteBuffer.allocateDirect(vertices.length * 4);
                  vbb.order(ByteOrder.nativeOrder());
     45           mVertexBuffer = vbb.asIntBuffer();
                  mVertexBuffer.put(vertices);
                  mVertexBuffer.position(0);
              }
```

Fixed vs. Floating Point

OpenGL ES provides fixed-point (integer) and floating-point interfaces for all its methods. The fixed-point methods end with the letter *x*, and the floating-point ones end with the letter *f*. For example, you can use either glColor4x() and glColor4f() to set the four components of a color.

A fixed-point number is scaled by 2^32, or 65,536. So, 32,768 in fixed point is equivalent to 0.5f. Put another way, the integral part uses the most significant two bytes of a four-byte int, while the fractional part uses the least significant two bytes. This is quite different from the way the native Android 2D library uses integers, so be careful.

In a simple example like this one, it doesn't matter whether you use fixed-point or floating-point arithmetic, so I use them interchangeably as convenient. Keep in mind, though, that some Android devices will not have floating-point hardware, so fixed point may be significantly faster. My advice is to code it first using floating point, because it's easier to program, and then optimize the slow parts using fixed point later if necessary.

```
50  public void draw(GL10 gl) {
        gl.glVertexPointer(3, GL10.GL_FIXED, 0, mVertexBuffer);

        gl.glColor4f(1, 1, 1, 1);
        gl.glNormal3f(0, 0, 1);
55      gl.glDrawArrays(GL10.GL_TRIANGLE_STRIP, 0, 4);
        gl.glNormal3f(0, 0, -1);
        gl.glDrawArrays(GL10.GL_TRIANGLE_STRIP, 4, 4);

        gl.glColor4f(1, 1, 1, 1);
60      gl.glNormal3f(-1, 0, 0);
        gl.glDrawArrays(GL10.GL_TRIANGLE_STRIP, 8, 4);
        gl.glNormal3f(1, 0, 0);
        gl.glDrawArrays(GL10.GL_TRIANGLE_STRIP, 12, 4);

65      gl.glColor4f(1, 1, 1, 1);
        gl.glNormal3f(0, 1, 0);
        gl.glDrawArrays(GL10.GL_TRIANGLE_STRIP, 16, 4);
        gl.glNormal3f(0, -1, 0);
        gl.glDrawArrays(GL10.GL_TRIANGLE_STRIP, 20, 4);
70  }
    }
```

The vertices array on line 18 defines the corners of the cube in fixed-point model coordinates (see the "Fixed vs. Floating Point" sidebar). Each face of a cube is a square, which consists of two triangles. We use a common OpenGL drawing mode called *triangle strips*. In this mode, we specify two starting points, and then after that every subsequent point defines a triangle with the previous two points. It's a quick way to get a lot of geometry pumped out to the graphics hardware in a hurry.

Note that each point has three coordinates (x, y, and z). The x and y axes point to the right and up, respectively, and the z axis points out of the screen toward the eye point.

In the draw method (line 50), we use the vertex buffer created in the constructor and draw six different runs of triangles (for the six sides of the cube). In a real program, you would want to combine the calls into one or two strips, because the fewer number of OpenGL calls you make, the faster your program will go.

Now let's use our new class in GLThread:

OpenGL/src/org/example/opengl/GLThread.java

```
private final GLCube cube = new GLCube();
private void drawFrame(GL10 gl) {
    // ... Draw the model
    cube.draw(gl);
}
```

Now if you run the program, you'll see the exciting image in Figure 10.3, on the next page. Well, it's more exciting than black.

10.6 Lights, Camera, ...

In real life you have light sources such as the sun, headlights, torches, or glowing lava pools. OpenGL lets you define up to eight light sources in your scene. There are two parts to lighting—a light and something to shine it on. Let's start with the light.

All 3D graphics libraries support three types of lighting:

- *Ambient*: A general glow that the light contributes to the entire scene, even to objects facing away from the light. It's important to have a little ambient light so you can pick out details even in the shadows.

Figure 10.3: DRAWING AN UNSHADED CUBE

- *Diffuse*: Soft directional lighting, as you might get from a fluorescent panel. Most of the light contributed to your scene will typically come from diffuse sources.

- *Specular*: Shiny light, usually from bright point sources. Combined with shiny materials, this gives you highlights (glints) that add realism.

A single light source can contribute all three types of light. These values go into a lighting equation that determines the color and brightness of each pixel on the screen.

The lighting is defined in the GLThread.init() method:

```
// Define the lighting
float lightAmbient[] = new float[] { 0.2f, 0.2f, 0.2f, 1 };
float lightDiffuse[] = new float[] { 1, 1, 1, 1 };
float[] lightPos = new float[] { 1, 1, 1, 1 };

gl.glEnable(GL10.GL_LIGHTING);
gl.glEnable(GL10.GL_LIGHT0);
gl.glLightfv(GL10.GL_LIGHT0, GL10.GL_AMBIENT, lightAmbient, 0);
gl.glLightfv(GL10.GL_LIGHT0, GL10.GL_DIFFUSE, lightDiffuse, 0);
gl.glLightfv(GL10.GL_LIGHT0, GL10.GL_POSITION, lightPos, 0);
```

In our code we define one light source at position (1, 1, 1). It's a white omnidirectional light that has a bright diffuse component and a dim ambient component. In this example, we're not using specular lighting.

Next, we need to tell OpenGL about the materials our cube is made of. Light reflects differently off different materials, such as metal, plastic, or paper. To simulate this in OpenGL, add this code in init() to define how the material reacts with the three types of light: ambient, diffuse, and specular:

```
// What is the cube made of?
float matAmbient[] = new float[] { 1, 1, 1, 1 };
float matDiffuse[] = new float[] { 1, 1, 1, 1 };
gl.glMaterialfv(GL10.GL_FRONT_AND_BACK, GL10.GL_AMBIENT,
        matAmbient, 0);
gl.glMaterialfv(GL10.GL_FRONT_AND_BACK, GL10.GL_DIFFUSE,
        matDiffuse, 0);
```

The object will appear to have a dull finish, as if it were made out of paper (see Figure 10.4, on the facing page). The top-right corner of the cube is closer to the light, so it appears brighter.

10.7 Action!

Up to now the cube has just been sitting there without moving. That's pretty boring, so let's make it move. To do that, we need to make a couple of changes to our init() and drawFrame() methods in GLThread.

Figure 10.4: LIGHTING THE SCENE

OpenGL/src/org/example/opengl/GLThread.java

```
private long startTime;
private void init(GL10 gl) {
    startTime = System.currentTimeMillis();
}
private void drawFrame(GL10 gl) {
    // ... Set rotation angle based on the time
    long elapsed = System.currentTimeMillis() - startTime;
    gl.glRotatef(elapsed * (30f / 1000f), 0, 1, 0);
    gl.glRotatef(elapsed * (15f / 1000f), 1, 0, 0);
}
```

This code rotates the cube a little bit every time through the main loop. Specifically, every second it rotates 30 degrees around the x axis and 15 degrees around the y axis. The result will be a nice, smooth, spinning cube (see Figure 10.5, on the next page).

Figure 10.5: ROTATING THE CUBE

Time-Based Animation

The first version of this example kept track of the current rotation angle and simply incremented it each time through the loop. Can you think of a reason why that was a bad idea?

Since Android can run on a variety of different devices, you can't predict how long it will take to draw a single frame. It might take half a second or 1/100th of a second. If you moved an object a fixed amount every frame, then on slow devices the object would move too slowly, and on fast devices it would move too fast. By tying the amount of movement to how much time has elapsed, you can achieve predictable movement on any device. Faster hardware will draw the animation more smoothly, but objects will get from A to B in the same amount of time.

10.8 Applying Texture

Although the scene is starting to look more interesting, nobody would mistake it for real life. Everyday objects have textures, like the rough surface of a brick wall or the gravel on a garden path. Do you own a laminated table? A wood laminate is just a photograph of wood grain that is glued on the surface of a less expensive material like plastic or particle board.

We're going to do the same thing to our cube using a picture. Unfortunately, the code to do this is fairly long. Don't worry if you don't understand it all right away.

OpenGL/src/org/example/opengl/GLCube.java

```
Line 1      private final IntBuffer mTextureBuffer;

            public GLCube() {
                int texCoords[] = {
5                       // FRONT
                        0, one, one, one, 0, 0, one, 0,
                        // BACK
                        one, one, one, 0, 0, one, 0, 0,
                        // LEFT
10                      one, one, one, 0, 0, one, 0, 0,
                        // RIGHT
                        one, one, one, 0, 0, one, 0, 0,
                        // TOP
                        one, 0, 0, 0, one, one, 0, one,
15                      // BOTTOM
                        0, 0, 0, one, one, 0, one, one, };
                // ...
                ByteBuffer tbb = ByteBuffer.allocateDirect(texCoords.length * 4);
                tbb.order(ByteOrder.nativeOrder());
20              mTextureBuffer = tbb.asIntBuffer();
                mTextureBuffer.put(texCoords);
                mTextureBuffer.position(0);
            }

25          static void loadTexture(GL10 gl, Context context, int resource) {
                Bitmap bmp = BitmapFactory.decodeResource(
                        context.getResources(), resource);

                ByteBuffer bb = extract(bmp);
30
                load(gl, bb, bmp.getWidth(), bmp.getHeight());
            }
```

```
      private static ByteBuffer extract(Bitmap bmp) {
35        ByteBuffer bb = ByteBuffer.allocateDirect(bmp.getHeight()
              * bmp.getWidth() * 4);
          bb.order(ByteOrder.BIG_ENDIAN);
          IntBuffer ib = bb.asIntBuffer();

40        // Convert ARGB -> RGBA
          for (int y = bmp.getHeight() - 1; y > -1; y--)
            for (int x = 0; x < bmp.getWidth(); x++) {
              int pix = bmp.getPixel(x, bmp.getHeight() - y - 1);
              // int alpha = ((pix >> 24) & 0xFF);
45            int red = ((pix >> 16) & 0xFF);
              int green = ((pix >> 8) & 0xFF);
              int blue = ((pix) & 0xFF);

              // Make up alpha for interesting effect
50            ib.put(red << 24 | green << 16 | blue << 8
                  | ((red + blue + green) / 3));
            }
          bb.position(0);
          return bb;
55      }

      private static void load(GL10 gl, ByteBuffer bb,
          int width, int height) {
        // Get a new texture name
60      int[] tmp_tex = new int[1];
        gl.glGenTextures(1, tmp_tex, 0);
        int tex = tmp_tex[0];

        // Load it up
65      gl.glBindTexture(GL10.GL_TEXTURE_2D, tex);
        gl.glTexImage2D(GL10.GL_TEXTURE_2D, 0, GL10.GL_RGBA,
            width, height, 0, GL10.GL_RGBA,
            GL10.GL_UNSIGNED_BYTE, bb);
        gl.glTexParameterx(GL10.GL_TEXTURE_2D,
70          GL10.GL_TEXTURE_MIN_FILTER, GL10.GL_LINEAR);
        gl.glTexParameterx(GL10.GL_TEXTURE_2D,
            GL10.GL_TEXTURE_MAG_FILTER, GL10.GL_LINEAR);
      }
    }
```

Most of the complexity comes from the need to convert a texture from an Android format (a Portable Network Graphics file) to a format that OpenGL can understand (packed integers with red, green, blue, and alpha values in that order). The extract() method (line 34) takes an Android Bitmap that we decoded using BitmapFactor.decodeResource() and copies it into a Java NIO ByteBuffer, doing the color conversion as it goes. The load() method (line 57) passes the buffer to OpenGL, which loads it onto a texture and prepares it for drawing.

Figure 10.6: APPLYING A TEXTURE

Next we need to tell OpenGL to use the texture coordinates. Add this line to the draw() method:

```
OpenGL/src/org/example/opengl/GLCube.java
gl.glTexCoordPointer(2, GL10.GL_FIXED, 0, mTextureBuffer);
```

And finally we need to call the loadTexture() method in GLThread.init():

```
OpenGL/src/org/example/opengl/GLThread.java
gl.glEnableClientState(GL10.GL_TEXTURE_COORD_ARRAY);
gl.glEnable(GL10.GL_TEXTURE_2D);

GLCube.loadTexture(gl, view.getContext(), R.drawable.android);
```

This code enables textures and texture coordinates and then calls our loadTexture() method, passing it the Activity context and resource ID so it can load the texture image.

R.drawable.android is a PNG file scaled down to 128 pixels square that I copied to res/drawable/android.png. You can find it in the downloadable code package that accompanies this book. Note the number 128 doesn't appear anywhere in the code, so you substitute a larger or smaller image easily. You want to keep it small, however, because the extract() method is painfully slow. Let's hope in a future release of Android that Google will provide an easier and faster way to do this.

You can see our progress so far in Figure 10.6, on the preceding page.

10.9 Peekaboo

Just for fun, let's make the cube partially transparent. Add this to GLThread.init():

OpenGL/src/org/example/opengl/GLThread.java

```
boolean SEE_THRU = true;
// ...
if (SEE_THRU) {
    gl.glDisable(GL10.GL_DEPTH_TEST);
    gl.glEnable(GL10.GL_BLEND);
    gl.glBlendFunc(GL10.GL_SRC_ALPHA, GL10.GL_ONE);
}
```

This turns off depth testing, because we want to see obscured objects as well as foreground ones. It also turns on a blending mode that lets the opacity of objects be based on their alpha channel. In GLCube, we defined the alpha channel as the average of the red, green, and blue values in the texture, which is a very rough way to calculate how bright the color is.[5] The net effect is that the back faces of the cube will appear through the darker parts of the front faces. For the final result, see Figure 10.7, on the next page.

I'll leave it to you to implement an option to turn that on and off. Try playing around with different blend modes to get cool effects.

---

5. Purists cringe at the sight of math like this, but these kinds of tricks are par for the course in 3D graphics. Most physical effects are too expensive to implement exactly, so estimates and shortcuts are common. Anyway, why limit yourself to what is possible in the physical world?

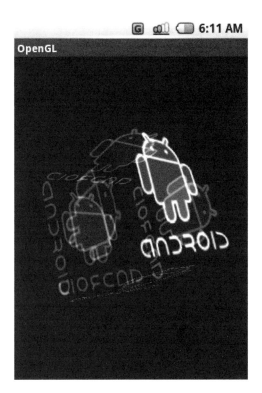

Figure 10.7: THE FINAL VERSION: A SEE-THROUGH CUBE

0.10 Fast-Forward >>

In this chapter, you learned how to use Android's 3D graphics library. Because Android uses the industry-standard OpenGL ES API, a wide variety of additional information is available if you want to learn more. In particular, I recommend the Javadoc for the JSR 239 API specification.[6]

What's next? Well, that's entirely up to you. You have all the tools you need, so go make something great!

---

6. http://java.sun.com/javame/reference/apis/jsr239

Part IV

Appendixes

Appendix A

Java vs. the Android Language and APIs

For the most part, Android programs are written in the Java language, and they use the Java 5 Standard Edition (SE) library APIs. I say "for the most part" because there are a few differences. This appendix highlights the differences between regular Java and what you'll find in Android. If you're already proficient in Java development on other platforms, you should take a close look to see what things you need to "unlearn."

A.1 Language Subset

Android uses a standard Java compiler to compile your source code into regular bytecodes and then translates those bytecodes into Dalvik instructions. Therefore, the entire Java language is supported, not just a subset. Compare this to the Google Web Toolkit (GWT), which has its own Java to JavaScript translator. By using the stock compiler and bytecodes, you don't even need to have the source code for libraries that you want to use in your applications.

Language Level

Android supports code compatible with Java Standard Edition 5 or earlier. Java 6 and 7 class formats and features are not yet supported but could be added in future releases.

Intrinsic Types

All Java intrinsic types including **byte, char, short, int, long, float, double**, Object, String, and arrays are supported. However, on current hardware commonly found in mobile devices, floating point is emulated. That means it's performed in software instead of hardware, making it much slower than normal. Simple operations on real numbers could take a millisecond to complete. Although occasional use is fine, do not use **float** or **double** in performance-critical code.

Multithreading and Synchronization

Multiple threads are supported by *time slicing*: giving each thread a few milliseconds to run and then performing a *context switch* to let another thread have a turn. Although Android will support any number of threads, in general you should use only one or two. One thread is dedicated for the main user interface (if you have one), and another thread is used for long-running operations such as calculations or network I/O.

The Dalvik VM implements the **synchronized** keyword and synchronization-related library methods such as Object.wait(), Object.notify(), and Object.notifyAll(). It also supports the java.util.concurrent package for more sophisticated algorithms. Use them as you would in any Java program to keep multiple threads from interfering with each other.

Reflection

Although the Android platform supports Java reflection, as a general rule you should not use it. The reason is simple performance: reflection is slow. Consider alternatives such as compile-time tools and preprocessors instead.

Finalization

The Dalvik VM supports object finalization during garbage collection just like regular Java VMs. However, most Java experts advise you not to rely on finalizers because you cannot predict when (or if) they will run. Instead of finalizers, use explicit close() or terminate() methods. Android is targeted toward resource-constrained hardware, so it's important that you release all resources as soon as you no longer need them.

A.2 Standard Library Subset

Android supports a relatively large subset of the Java Standard Edition 5.0 library. Some things were left out because they simply didn't make sense (such as printing), and others were omitted because better APIs are available that are specific to Android (such as user interfaces).

Supported

The following standard packages are supported in Android. Consult the Java 2 Platform Standard Edition 5.0 API documentation[1] for information on how to use them:

- java.awt.font: A few constants for Unicode and fonts
- java.io: File and stream I/O
- java.lang (except java.lang.management): Language and exception support
- java.math: Big numbers, rounding, precision
- java.net: Network I/O, URLs, sockets
- java.nio: File and channel I/O
- java.security: Authorization, certificates, public keys
- java.sql: Database interfaces
- java.text: Formatting, natural language, collation
- java.util (including java.util.concurrent): Lists, maps, sets, arrays, collections
- javax.crypto: Ciphers, public keys
- javax.microedition.khronos: OpenGL graphics (from Java Micro Edition)
- javax.net: Socket factories, SSL
- javax.security (except javax.security.auth.kerberos, javax.security.auth.spi, and javax.security.sasl)
- javax.sql (except javax.sql.rowset): More database interfaces
- javax.xml.parsers: XML parsing
- org.w3c.dom (but not subpackages): DOM nodes and elements
- org.xml.sax: Simple API for XML

Note that although the regular Java SQL database APIs (JDBC) are included, you don't use them to access local SQLite databases. Use the android.database APIs instead (see Chapter 9, *Putting SQL to Work*, on page 161).

---

1. http://java.sun.com/j2se/1.5.0/docs/api

Not Supported

These packages, normally part of the Java 2 Platform Standard Edition, are *not* supported by Android:

- java.applet
- java.awt
- java.beans
- java.lang.management
- java.rmi
- javax.accessibility
- javax.activity
- javax.imageio
- javax.management
- javax.naming
- javax.print
- javax.rmi
- javax.security.auth.kerberos
- javax.security.auth.spi
- javax.security.sasl
- javax.sound
- javax.swing
- javax.transaction
- javax.xml (except javax.xml.parsers)
- org.ietf.*
- org.omg.*
- org.w3c.dom.* (subpackages)

A.3 Third-Party Libraries

In addition to the standard libraries listed earlier, the Android SDK comes with a number of third-party libraries for your convenience:

- org.apache.http: HTTP authentication, cookies, methods, and protocol
- org.json: JavaScript Object Notation
- org.xml.sax: XML parsing
- org.xmlpull.v1: XML parsing

Appendix B
Bibliography

[Bur05]   Ed Burnette. *Eclipse IDE Pocket Guide*. O'Reilly & Associates, Inc, Sebastopol, CA, 2005.

[Gen06]   Jonathan Gennick. *SQL Pocket Guide*. O'Reilly Media, Inc., Sebastopol, CA, second edition, 2006.

[Goe06]   Brian Goetz. *Java Concurrency in Practice*. Addison-Wesley, Reading, MA, 2006.

[Owe06]   Mike Owens. *The Definitive Guide to SQLite*. Apress, Berkeley, CA, 2006.

Index

Web 2.0

Welcome to the Web, version 2.0. You need some help to tame the wild technologies out there. Start with *Prototype and script.aculo.us*, a book about two libraries that will make your JavaScript life much easier.

See how to reach the largest possible web audience with *The Accessible Web*.

Prototype and script.aculo.us

Tired of getting swamped in the nitty-gritty of cross-browser, Web 2.0–grade JavaScript? Get back in the game with Prototype and script.aculo.us, two extremely popular JavaScript libraries that make it a walk in the park. Be it Ajax, drag and drop, autocompletion, advanced visual effects, or many other great features, all you need is to write one or two lines of script that look so good they could almost pass for Ruby code!

Prototype and script.aculo.us: You Never Knew JavaScript Could Do This!
Christophe Porteneuve
(330 pages) ISBN: 1-934356-01-8. $34.95
http://pragprog.com/titles/cppsu

Design Accessible Web Sites

The 2000 U.S. Census revealed that 12% of the population is severely disabled. Sometime in the next two decades, one in five Americans will be older than 65. Section 508 of the Americans with Disabilities Act requires your website to provide *equivalent access* to all potential users. But beyond the law, it is both good manners and good business to make your site accessible to everyone. This book shows you how to design sites that excel for all audiences.

Design Accessible Web Sites: 36 Keys to Creating Content for All Audiences and Platforms
Jeremy Sydik
(304 pages) ISBN: 978-1-9343560-2-9. $34.95
http://pragprog.com/titles/jsaccess

Getting It Done

Start with the habits of an agile developer and use the team practices of successful agile teams, and your project will fly over the finish line.

Practices of an Agile Developer

Agility is all about using feedback to respond to change. Learn how to • apply the principles of agility throughout the software development process • establish and maintain an agile working environment • deliver what users really want • use personal agile techniques for better coding and debugging • use effective collaborative techniques for better teamwork • move to an agile approach

**Practices of an Agile Developer:
Working in the Real World**
Venkat Subramaniam and Andy Hunt
(189 pages) ISBN: 0-9745140-8-X. $29.95
http://pragprog.com/titles/pad

Ship It!

Page after page of solid advice, all tried and tested in the real world. This book offers a collection of tips that show you what tools a successful team has to use, and how to use them well. You'll get quick, easy-to-follow advice on modern techniques and when they should be applied. **You need this book if:** • you're frustrated at lack of progress on your project. • you want to make yourself and your team more valuable. • you've looked at methodologies such as Extreme Programming (XP) and felt they were too, well, extreme. • you've looked at the Rational Unified Process (RUP) or CMM/I methods and cringed at the learning curve and costs. • **you need to get software out the door without excuses.**

Ship It! A Practical Guide to Successful Software Projects
Jared Richardson and Will Gwaltney
(200 pages) ISBN: 0-9745140-4-7. $29.95
http://pragprog.com/titles/prj

Get Groovy

Expand your horizons with Groovy, and tame the wild Java VM.

Programming Groovy

Programming Groovy will help you learn the necessary fundamentals of programming in Groovy. You'll see how to use Groovy to do advanced programming techniques, including meta programming, builders, unit testing with mock objects, processing XML, working with databases and creating your own domain-specific languages (DSLs).

Programming Groovy: Dynamic Productivity for the Java Developer
Venkat Subramaniam
(320 pages) ISBN: 978-1-9343560-9-8. $34.95
http://pragprog.com/titles/vslg

Groovy Recipes

See how to speed up nearly every aspect of the development process using *Groovy Recipes*. Groovy makes mundane file management tasks like copying and renaming files trivial. Reading and writing XML has never been easier with XmlParsers and XmlBuilders. Breathe new life into arrays, maps, and lists with a number of convenience methods. Learn all about Grails, and go beyond HTML into the world of Web Services: REST, JSON, Atom, Podcasting, and much, much more.

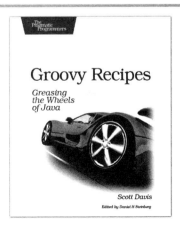

Groovy Recipes: Greasing the Wheels of Java
Scott Davis
(264 pages) ISBN: 978-0-9787392-9-4. $34.95
http://pragprog.com/titles/sdgrvr

The Pragmatic Bookshelf

Available in paperback and DRM-free PDF, our titles are here to help you stay on top of your game. The following are in print as of December 2008; be sure to check our website at pragprog.com for newer titles.

Title	Year	ISBN	Pages
Advanced Rails Recipes: 84 New Ways to Build Stunning Rails Apps	2008	9780978739225	464
Agile Retrospectives: Making Good Teams Great	2006	9780977616640	200
Agile Web Development with Rails: Second Edition	2006	9780977616633	719
Augmented Reality: A Practical Guide	2008	9781934356036	328
Behind Closed Doors: Secrets of Great Management	2005	9780976694021	192
Best of Ruby Quiz	2006	9780976694076	304
Core Animation for Mac OS X and the iPhone: Creating Compelling Dynamic User Interfaces	2008	9781934356104	200
Data Crunching: Solve Everyday Problems using Java, Python, and More	2005	9780974514079	208
Deploying Rails Applications: A Step-by-Step Guide	2008	9780978739201	280
Design Accessible Web Sites: 36 Keys to Creating Content for All Audiences and Platforms	2007	9781934356029	336
Desktop GIS: Mapping the Planet with Open Source Tools	2008	9781934356067	368
Developing Facebook Platform Applications with Rails	2008	9781934356128	200
Enterprise Integration with Ruby	2006	9780976694069	360
Enterprise Recipes with Ruby and Rails	2008	9781934356234	416
Everyday Scripting with Ruby: for Teams, Testers, and You	2007	9780977616619	320
FXRuby: Create Lean and Mean GUIs with Ruby	2008	9781934356074	240
From Java To Ruby: Things Every Manager Should Know	2006	9780976694090	160
GIS for Web Developers: Adding Where to Your Web Applications	2007	9780974514093	275
Google Maps API, V2: Adding Where to Your Applications	2006	PDF-Only	83
Groovy Recipes: Greasing the Wheels of Java	2008	9780978739294	264
Interface Oriented Design	2006	9780976694052	240
Learn to Program	2006	9780976694045	176
Manage It! Your Guide to Modern Pragmatic Project Management	2007	9780978739249	360

Continued on next page

Title	Year	ISBN	Pages
Mastering Dojo: JavaScript and Ajax Tools for Great Web Experiences	2008	9781934356111	568
My Job Went to India: 52 Ways to Save Your Job	2005	9780976694014	208
No Fluff Just Stuff 2006 Anthology	2006	9780977616664	240
No Fluff Just Stuff 2007 Anthology	2007	9780978739287	320
Practices of an Agile Developer	2006	9780974514086	189
Pragmatic Ajax: A Web 2.0 Primer	2006	9780976694083	296
Pragmatic Project Automation: How to Build, Deploy, and Monitor Java Applications	2004	9780974514031	176
Pragmatic Thinking and Learning: Refactor Your Wetware	2008	9781934356050	288
Pragmatic Unit Testing in C# with NUnit	2007	9780977616671	176
Pragmatic Unit Testing in Java with JUnit	2003	9780974514017	160
Pragmatic Version Control using CVS	2003	9780974514000	176
Pragmatic Version Control using Subversion	2006	9780977616657	248
Programming Erlang: Software for a Concurrent World	2007	9781934356005	536
Programming Groovy: Dynamic Productivity for the Java Developer	2008	9781934356098	320
Programming Ruby: The Pragmatic Programmers' Guide, Second Edition	2004	9780974514055	864
Prototype and script.aculo.us: You Never Knew JavaScript Could Do This!	2007	9781934356012	448
Rails Recipes	2006	9780977616602	350
Rails for .NET Developers	2008	9781934356203	300
Rails for Java Developers	2007	9780977616695	336
Rails for PHP Developers	2008	9781934356043	432
Rapid GUI Development with QtRuby	2005	PDF-Only	83
Release It! Design and Deploy Production-Ready Software	2007	9780978739218	368
Scripted GUI Testing with Ruby	2008	9781934356180	192
Ship it! A Practical Guide to Successful Software Projects	2005	9780974514048	224
Stripes ...And Java Web Development Is Fun Again	2008	9781934356210	375
TextMate: Power Editing for the Mac	2007	9780978739232	208
The Definitive ANTLR Reference: Building Domain-Specific Languages	2007	9780978739256	384
ThoughtWorks Anthology	2008	9781934356142	240
Ubuntu Kung Fu: Tips, Tricks, Hints, and Hacks	2008	9781934356227	400

The Pragmatic Bookshelf

The Pragmatic Bookshelf features books written by developers for developers. The titles continue the well-known Pragmatic Programmer style and continue to garner awards and rave reviews. As development gets more and more difficult, the Pragmatic Programmers will be there with more titles and products to help you stay on top of your game.

Visit Us Online

Hello Android's Home Page
http://pragprog.com/titles/eband
Source code from this book, errata, and other resources. Come give us feedback, too!

Register for Updates
http://pragprog.com/updates
Be notified when updates and new books become available.

Join the Community
http://pragprog.com/community
Read our weblogs, join our online discussions, participate in our mailing list, interact with our wiki, and benefit from the experience of other Pragmatic Programmers.

New and Noteworthy
http://pragprog.com/news
Check out the latest pragmatic developments in the news.

Save on the PDF

Save on the PDF version of this book. Owning the paper version of this book entitles you to purchase the PDF version at a terrific discount. The PDF is great for carrying around on your laptop. It's hyperlinked, has color, and is fully searchable.

Buy it now at pragprog.com/coupon.

Contact Us

Phone Orders:	1-800-699-PROG (+1 919 847 3884)
Online Orders:	www.pragprog.com/catalog
Customer Service:	orders@pragprog.com
Non-English Versions:	translations@pragprog.com
Pragmatic Teaching:	academic@pragprog.com
Author Proposals:	proposals@pragprog.com